D1271425

VIC BRADEN'S

Laugh and Win at Doubles

ALSO BY VIC BRADEN

Vic Braden's Tennis for the Future
(with Bill Bruns)

Teaching Children Tennis the Vic Braden Way
(with Bill Bruns)

Vic Braden's Quick Fixes
(with Bill Bruns)

Vic Braden's Mental Tennis
(with Robert Wool)

VIC BRADEN'S

Laugh and Win at Doubles

VIC BRADEN and
BILL BRUNS

Little, Brown and Company
Boston New York Toronto London

First Edition

Library of Congress Cataloging-in-Publication Data

Braden, Vic.

Vic Braden's laugh and win at doubles / by Vic Braden and Bill Bruns. — 1st ed.

p. cm.

ISBN 0-316-10519-8 (alk. paper)

1. Tennis — Doubles. I. Bruns, Bill. II. Title.

GV1002.8.B73 1996

796.34'2 — dc20 95-41050

10 9 8 7 6 5 4 3 2 1

RRD-OH

Designed by Barbara Werden

Published simultaneously in Canada by
Little, Brown & Company (Canada) Limited

Printed in the United States of America

From Vic Braden:
To Ruth Moore and Betty Morse, a great doubles team

From Bill Bruns:
To my wife, Pam, my partner for life

Contents

Acknowledgments

A good group of pals to have when you need to start a sports research project . . . thanks: Dr. Gideon Ariel, Dr. Paul Braden, Dr. J. E. Broadwell, Dr. Howard Brody, Dr. Ray Brown, Dr. Charles Dillman, Dr. James Fallon, Dr. Richard Haier, Dr. Michael Holden, Dr. Patrick Keating, Dr. Hans Liepmann, Dr. Arnold Mandell, Jon Niednagel, Dr. Ann Penny, Dr. Frank Pollick, Dr. Charles Ribak, Dr. Richard Schmidt, and Dr. Andrei Vorobiev.

And to all those great players on the back of this book, who made the game exciting to research. And to my staff members who have worn a path carrying heavy camera equipment to the research scene. We also greatly appreciated the expertise and support of the following people, as we conceived and produced this book: our agent, John Boswell; our editor in chief, Bill Phillips; our guiding editor, Catherine Crawford; our copyeditor, Pamela Marshall; our designer, Barbara Werden; and three of the people who read the manuscript — Charlotte Gumbrell, Mary Ley, and Kay Ley.

VIC BRADEN'S

Laugh and Win at Doubles

The "Laugh and Win" Philosophy

WHEN I started the junior program at the Kramer Club on the Palos Verdes peninsula in the mid-1960s, I had youngsters who were truly hungry to become outstanding tennis players. Athletic and competitive, they came out every day after school to practice and would play all weekend whenever they could steal court time from the adults. Soon they were winning junior tournaments all around Southern California, and eventually one of them — Tracy Austin — would win the U.S. Open singles title and Wimbledon mixed doubles with her brother John. When I left in 1970 to open my tennis college, Robert Landsdorp took over the program and did a great job, but I feel I instilled a lasting spirit in all the Kramer Club kids of that era by emphasizing a "laugh and win" approach to the game. "We worked unbelievably hard," Tracy later recalled, "but we also laughed hard and we always had a lot of fun."

Looking back now, I realize that when I coined my motto many years ago, I perhaps should have reversed the emphasis, since many players regard laughing on the tennis court as secondary in importance to winning. In fact, you may share the attitude I encounter everywhere, including at my tennis college, where students concede: "I'll laugh, Vic, after I learn to win."

Unfortunately, too many people bring that "winning is the bottom line" philosophy not only to tennis, but to other individual and team sports — both as participants and as spectators. Yet I will continue to campaign on behalf of my belief that the laughing can even come before the winning, because that's still what sports should be about: Play as hard and as well as

1 John Austin and his younger sister Tracy celebrate their mixed-doubles championship at Wimbledon in 1980.

you can and have fun doing it; the winning will fall into place.

I like the spirit expressed by a New York writer who took heart after his friend's death by recalling the friend's contributions to their favorite sport. He wrote, "On the tennis court, John was intense and involved. Pleasure radiated from him; but, across the net from him, you'd catch something steely in his gaze that made you understand what you were up against. Mostly, he won, and if you were lucky enough to be his doubles partner that day, you felt better about yourself when you came off the court. You wanted him back next time."

I also support the sentiments of Gigi Fernandez, who has partnered Russia's Natalia (now Natasha) Zvereva in recent years to form a team that won eight Grand Slam events from 1991 through 1994. Before they joined up, Gigi had played with Czech Jana Novotna; and she later told Cindy Hahn of *Tennis* magazine, "Jana was so serious and sour, just never smiled, and that was very hard for me, because I play my best when I'm having fun. With Natalia, I can do that." Jerry Crowe of the *Los Angeles Times* later quoted Gigi: "That's very important to me — to be able to have fun on the court because I play most relaxed when I'm having fun. Natalia has a fun personality. She likes to have fun on the court, and she jokes. And she is emotional, like I am. I think that's why we win so much — because we somehow find a

2 Court hogs kill a good doubles team. *(Photo: John G. Zimmerman)*

way to have fun even when the pressure is just ridiculous or things are just not going our way."

This is the spirit of my "laugh and win" philosophy, and by focusing on strokes, tactics, and psychology, this book will give you a detailed game plan for playing winning doubles at every level — while also having fun.

I savor doubles as a challenging adventure for even the singles purist, a game that should be competitive *and* enjoyable, not a war. Unfortunately, there's something about the game that can bring out the absolute worst in people, transforming the mildest of men and the sweetest of women into barracudas. Friendships and marriages creak under the strain, especially when on-court partnerships are poorly conceived or become barely disguised rivalries.

Why is it that doubles — especially mixed doubles — can turn so easily into all-out combat when the competition heats up?

One explanation is the psychological dynamics at work on the court. Your weaknesses and your mistakes are more on display in front of more people than in singles. Every goof is magnified. You're performing not only in front of two opponents, but a partner who may try hard to mask his emotions but can't conceal his body language when you dump a break point into the net. If you're playing poorly, you not only feel upset with yourself, but you also feel guilty for the way you're undermining your team's chances.

Another factor may be the inability of two players to share responsibility on the court and respect one another's playing abilities. When one partner thinks he or

3 The server is asking for trouble by having her partner begin the point inside the outlined imaginary four-foot box in the doubles alley. Instead, he should be positioned on an imaginary "X" in the middle of the service box, ready to break in any direction for the returner's shot.

she should take charge of the situation, regardless of the tactics in good doubles — or their respective playing abilities — the result is usually a court hog who spoils much of the fun and undermines the team's performance.

We can all recognize, for example, that classic husband-and-wife team where the man prepares to serve at the beginning of the match. He takes his wife up to the net and says, "Darling, big match today, right? If we win, we'll be king and queen of Pismo Beach. Now, you are so valuable and you volley so well that I'm going to put you in this all-time important spot" — a four-foot cubicle in the alley, right in front of the net. When he walks away he says, "And don't forget, hold the racket up in front of your face."

Subconsciously, what he is really saying to her is this: "Look, I can play these guys alone. If I could, I would put you on the bench, but it wouldn't look too good to our neighbors."

Of course, as I emphasize everywhere I travel, a doubles team wins with *teamwork;* both players have equally important roles and both must contribute. The husband (or wife) we recognize above thinks he's going to make his spouse famous by running all over the court to save every point, but an interesting thing happens: He starts running out of oxygen while she keeps getting all the shots. If she's aggressive up at the net and can volley, she'll be the hero — not her husband — because she'll put fantastic pressure on the other team.

Why Doubles Can be Appreciated

I've always loved tennis doubles as a player, a coach, and a spectator; and I've long championed what it offers at every level. All the action, the fun, and psychology of singles is multiplied by two, and you can make it as social or cutthroat at you want. I grew up admiring Donald Budge, a great singles and doubles player, and what he had to say about doubles still holds true today: "For sheer enjoyment, thrills, and satisfaction you can't beat a good game of doubles between two evenly matched teams of the first rank. There is more fun in doubles, both for the players and the spectators."

Despite the popularity of that crazed and refreshing team of Luke and Murphy Jensen, doubles remains an outcast event for most of the top pros. They can make a lot more money concentrating on singles and they prefer not to complicate their lives and risk injury by entering a tournament's doubles competition. Although he certainly has the requisite skills (as revealed by his doubles play against the Russians when the United States won the Davis Cup in 1995), Wimbledon and U.S. Open champ Pete Sampras explained why he skips doubles: "I need that time during a tournament to rest for singles."

Fortunately, doubles is thriving at the club and recreational level as the tennis boomers of the 1970s embrace middle age and as tennis leagues proliferate around the country. In fact, doubles has clearly become the game of choice for millions of club and recreational players in the 1990s. The Alta League in Atlanta alone has more than 70,000 members playing every week, with the emphasis on doubles (since the typical team-versus-team format features two singles and four doubles matches). Leagues not only provide year-round competition but also the ongoing motivation to become a better doubles player, as an individual and with a teammate. Industry surveys show that "being part of a team" — playing with a partner and having other teammates — is a high priority and motivation for people playing the game.

Still, while tennis is thriving at the high school and college levels, many young people feel that doubles is a game to save for when they turn 50, which is an unfair assessment of what this game demands in tennis skills. You need only watch the over-70 and over-80 tournaments around the country to see men and women serve and volley like teenagers, in singles and doubles alike.

Happily for all of us who are campaigning for the sport's future growth, doubles is popular at the school level, where there are 5,600 college and 18,500 high school programs, most of them having teams for both sexes. I've noticed that many of the young singles players drop out when they grow older, but the doubles aficionados practically go to their grave before they give up the sport.

Numerous reasons account for the popularity of doubles, starting with the simple joy of playing with another person against two other people, all of whom are intent on winning and having some fun. Just as in singles, each point starts with the serve and then proceeds until one team hits an irretrievable shot inside the opponents' boundaries or is unable to return an opponent's shot inside those boundaries. The points pile up just as in singles — for example, 15-love, 30-love, 30-all, deuce, ad in (server's advantage), and ad out (receiver's advantage) — and lead to game, set, and match. And afterward the usual scenario goes like this: The winners are congratulating themselves for having figured out the best system to play, and the losers are busy working on a new plan to defeat their opponents the next time they play. That's the cycle that has kept tennis alive for several centuries.

Players coming over from singles soon realize that doubles offers a better opportunity to improve one's basic shots — the serve, service return, volley, overhead, and lob — under greater pressure than in singles.* Since both teams are continually trying to control the net in good doubles, the game makes fewer demands on basic ground strokes from the baseline and focuses attention on the server, the service returner (he must keep his shot away from the net person, which narrows his hitting options), and everybody's volleying ability once the point begins. Meanwhile, if a team is going to play doubles "correctly" (meaning, the prevailing style of play in leagues and tournament competition), each player must know how to advance to the net, volley, retreat against lobs, and hit overheads. In 1990, noted Peter Bodo in *Tennis* magazine, Aranxta Sanchez Vicario of Spain was "all defense" as a singles player, and her coach, Mike Estep, challenged her to improve her net play and acquire a more aggressive attitude by playing doubles. Her next coach, Sven Groeneveld, also emphasized that she needed to "explore the net" to reach the top in singles. Happily for Vicario, she had the physical talent for doubles — quick hands, good hand-eye coordination, and a natural ability to move — and in 1994, she won not only the U.S. Open singles title but women's doubles as well, teamed with Jana Novotna.

Another important attraction of doubles is the fact that it's fun to play as a team, sharing the camaraderie, the workload, and the responsibility for winning and losing with another person. Even if you play like a toad all day and rarely hit a good shot, you can always say, "If only my partner had played well, we would have beaten those bums." Or if you've played poorly but your partner was terrific and your team won, you can talk about how "we" won the match.

Most people also appreciate the fact that they're covering basically nine fewer feet of court than they would be in singles (the doubles court being 36 feet wide versus 27 in singles). This means that on a given day when you're playing lousy, you can be rescued by a partner who is able to cover most of the court, and, conversely, you can bail out your partner on his off-day. With less court to cover in doubles, you can focus more on strategy and the intricacies of teamwork, while learning something new every time you play by observing the different playing styles of various opponents from match to match. Moreover, if you and your partner can play your positions correctly — staying about 10 to 12 feet apart as you cover the court as a team — opponents have very narrow paths in which they can hit the ball past you (see photo 5). And if you can anticipate shots, speed afoot is not as important as in singles. Many

* The various tennis shots and terms are described in the glossary and at appropriate points in the text.

A

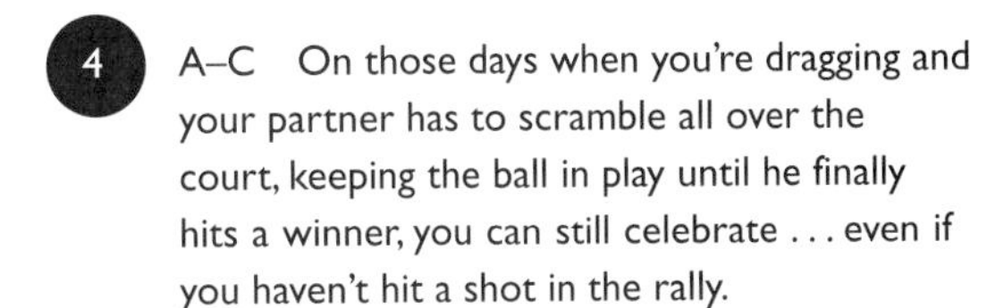

4 A–C On those days when you're dragging and your partner has to scramble all over the court, keeping the ball in play until he finally hits a winner, you can still celebrate . . . even if you haven't hit a shot in the rally.

B

C

people who aren't as fast on their feet as most of their singles opponents but have good court sense and anticipation often become excellent doubles players. People with agility and quick reactions can overcome slow feet in doubles because they are now having to patrol less court and their success is not as dependent on speed as it is in singles.

Yet another appeal of doubles is the fact that men and women, parents and kids, seniors and teens can all have fun playing together and against each other on a more equal basis than in singles. Handled properly, a doubles partnership offers parents a great way to have positive interaction with their children on the tennis court — creating a relationship that can extend for many years and prove quite rewarding.

A good example is the father-son team from Pacific Palisades, Ernie and Chris Schoop, who have been playing national tournaments together since the mid-'70s, once ranking as high as number two in the nation. Each has had an individual career (Chris as the number-one doubles player at UC Berkeley for three years), but they both admit that there is nothing quite like taking the court as a father-son team.

"One of the most exciting moments I've ever had was when we won the [national] Indoors," Chris said. "It's a sensation found in no other competition," Ernie added, because "maybe you want to win for the family name." Chris agreed. "As much as I try to keep a lighthearted attitude, I find myself wanting to win for my dad."

Making the Transition from Singles to Doubles

Are you a terrific singles player whose game seems to fall apart the moment you are part of a strong doubles foursome? One fundamental reason may be that you don't volley well enough to play good doubles; you're a hero on the baseline but a klutz at the net. Also, players with shorter swings normally make better doubles players because there isn't as much time for long flowing swings as there is in singles. A third explanation could be that players who love extremely fast action normally excel in doubles, in contrast to players who prefer to camp on the baseline and try to win from there. This doesn't work too well because there is less territory in which to manipulate two smart opponents. Fourth, perhaps you have been saddled with a succession of partners whose skills — and weaknesses — haven't meshed well with your particular talents and shortcomings.

More likely, however, the reason you may be a world-beater in singles but a pushover in doubles has to do mainly with your mental attitude toward doubles. You must accept the fact, first of all, that singles and doubles are different games within tennis, calling for different approaches. This sounds obvious, I know, yet I find that many people don't fully appreciate just how different the two games are and, consequently, what this demands of them as a player.

In singles, for example, depending upon whom you're playing, you can more often get away with little glitches in your game than in doubles. If your opponent never comes to the net behind her serve, you don't have to worry as much about where you're returning the ball, just so long as you keep it deep. In doubles, you must keep your service return away from the net person, which greatly narrows your hitting options. Then, too, if you're quick on your feet, you can often overcome poorly executed shots in singles by covering your opponent's subsequent shot with retrieving ability. Little such luck in doubles. And if you're playing singles against a baseliner whose basic strategy is to wait for you to make the first error, you can be much less concerned about where to aim. Just pop the ball back with the message "Here's one more chance for you to finish second in a field of two" and hope that you can continue to outlast him as you think about the beach in between shots. This approach simply won't work well in doubles against strong competition. You must concentrate on every ball you hit because a weak shot will almost always be returned and cost your team dearly.

Psychology is a second important consideration here. Quite possibly, despite your singles ability, you may not be as temperamentally suited for doubles. Remember, you have to share the responsibility — and the glory. And that's a tough assignment for many players, particularly those who bring highly egocentric personalities to the court. They savor the spotlight when they make the big shots and have little patience with a partner who misses the shot that would have won the set. People who play singles all the time are always in control of their situation and their destiny, and, thus, often have trouble learning and accepting what it means to give in doubles.

For example, in doubles you should give way to a partner who has priority on a shot (even if he's hitting on your side of the court); you should give praise, even when praise isn't forthcoming; you have to give support to a partner when nothing is going right for your team; and you have to live with yourself when you make the error that costs your team the game or the set. In short, from a psychological perspective, doubles provides opportunities for "giving" to a partner who needs support, while singles is more about one person wanting it all.

Beyond attitude, there's an even more basic adjustment you must make when shifting from singles to doubles, and that's in the way you think. Doubles is much more of a thinking game once the ball is in play, in the sense that you must become something of a chess player, anticipating the other team's moves and shots, because you have less time to make conscious decisions than in singles.

The Growing Accuracy and Value of Brain Typing

I have a friend, Jonathan P. Niednagel, who is in demand as a consultant to college and professional sports teams and athletes. His specialty is Brain Typing and how it can be used to identify various personality and motor traits in people, for use by coaches, front offices, and executive suites as they hire and evaluate athletes and employees. Drawing on his vast, accumulated knowledge of how an individual's mind/brain works in relation to his or her performance (and suitability) in a particular sport or profession, Jon has expanded on Dr. Carl Jung's 16 different brain types by highlighting the mental *and* motor skills of each type. He has also published his own book, *Your Best Sport: How to Choose and Play It,* which details how Brain Typing works and how it can be applied by individuals to various sports.

In terms of my sport, and specifically doubles, he notes,

> The more that people can understand about Brain Typing, the more useful it can be — if it's nothing more than picking the right doubles partner or understanding why the captain of the tennis team is so unlikable. But I'm confident that people can learn to use Brain Typing to understand themselves better and to gain insights into the people they are competing against, which will lead to improved performance and greater confidence as tennis players.
>
> For example, if Martha is an "ISFJ" (*I*ntrovert, *S*ensate, *F*eeler, *J*udges), she has a harder time ruling out "trash talk" or psyching efforts by the opposing team, especially since she is relational and it's important to her that everyone get along on both sides of the net. Knowing this about herself from a Brain Typing perspective should help her self-understanding as a tennis player. The other implication, of course, is that when a person gets into Brain Typing and can begin to read individual types, he can figure out his opponents and thus gain insights that can help him know how to get at their Achilles' heel, psychologically.
>
> A big issue with Brain Typing is to realize the possibilities, that if your partner acts a certain way and you know

the brain type, you can say to this person: "Here's what I know about you. . . . You have a tendency to do this, this and this, and when that happens, the result is this, this and this. So go ahead and be yourself, but I am hopeful that both of us can learn from one another's strengths."

It's so important just being aware of other people's brain types and your own brain type — how you act (mentally and physically), your vulnerabilities, how you process information, and how you respond to emotional situations.

In chapter 2, I'll offer some important insights that Brain Typing can provide when you seek out a compatible partner and as you analyze your current doubles partnership.

In this book, which is drawn from more than 50 years of teaching, researching, and coaching tennis, I will "coach" you to play better doubles and have more fun than you've ever had out on the court. Pay attention to the essential principles (described in the next chapter) that I always emphasize in my teaching and you may discover that you'll be more eager to play doubles than singles. Just make sure your partner's in on the plan.

The Essentials of Good Doubles

WHEREVER I travel in the tennis world, whether to conduct clinics, speak at symposiums, or watch tournaments, I'm reminded that the principles of good doubles remain pretty much unchanged through the years:

1. Play with **enthusiasm**.
2. **Attack** at every opportunity, striving to get as close to the net as possible for your next shot.
3. The team that **controls the net** controls the point.
4. Keep the ball **away from the netman.**
5. Force your opponents to **hit up** (from below net level), so that your team can move up and **hit down** with an easier volley or overhead.
6. **Move together** as a team.
7. Don't let your feet fall asleep; **be moving all the time** — running, stretching, anticipating.
8. The person **closer to the net has priority** on any shot that he can reach.
9. Constantly **communicate** with your partner.
10. Treasure your team's ability to **keep the ball in play**; even a good lob forces the opponents to win the point rather than be given a point.
11. Have fun, **laugh your head off,** and try to learn along the way.

Indeed, while we all play doubles for different reasons, the tactics, strategy, and crucial skills never really change — just their relative importance.

A

B

C

5 A–C When a team is hitting from the baseline, there's very little room to drive the ball past opponents who are positioned properly, 10 to 12 feet apart. The targets are very small and dangerous. Also notice how the opponents try to remain the same distance apart when they shift from one sideline to the other to cover shots.

For example, our studies have found that accumulated racket improvements in recent years have given top players about 35 percent more power in off-center hits than with previous equipment. This means that even when the pros miss the sweet spot on their strings, they produce fewer "floppy" shots and can still hit with real power. As a result, the ball is traveling fast all the time in big-time doubles, and this underscores the importance of reading the opponent's intentions as he goes to hit, perceiving what's going to happen with his shot, and then moving toward the ball with a fast first step. The same relative importance of these skills applies all the way down the food chain.

Knowing the key requirements of good doubles should help confirm whether or not you're currently paired up with the right person while providing many specific questions to ask — and resolve — the next time you seek a partner (which I'll explore in chapter 2).

1. Always think ATTACK! Playing doubles "the right way," in the sense of trying to defeat a stronger team, begins

6 The team that gains control of the net is usually just a shot away from winning the point.

with a basic premise: *The battle is won at the net.* Relative strengths in serving and returning serve are critical, of course, but ultimately the team that controls the net wins the big points and takes control of the match (see photo 6).

The best doubles teams are those in which each player is constantly striving to go forward and is looking for that opportunity as he hits and as he studies the opposing team's intentions. Baseline players, in club doubles, can often stay back and win with scrambling ability, great lobs, consistency, and unbelievable patience. In fact, their living rooms are often filled with trophies because their opponents make so many errors. But in topflight tennis, a defensive team like this can rarely beat a good net-playing team.

Why is it so important to gain control of the fortress?

Well, first of all, your team has a better chance to end the point quickly when you and your partner are up at the net together, 10 to 12 feet apart. As photo 7 shows, this opens up the opponents' court and puts each of you in a position to hit sharply angled volleys or overheads for outright winners.

A second advantage is that the closer your team can approach the net, the more you will increase your opponents' anxiety level. The hitter will either see you rushing forward or know that you're already

7 When a doubles team can move forward from the "X," they gain much sharper volleying angles.

8 When a player must bend low to volley the ball from below the level of the net tape, he must raise the ball, giving the opponents a high-volley opportunity.

perched up there, ready to hit a putaway, and he'll know he must execute — right now! — or the point's over.

Third, by closing in on the net, your team drastically narrows the angles at which your opponents can safely aim the ball past you from the baseline. They must thread the needle with a drive — through a potential opening of only about one degree between the two of you — or attempt a lob.

Fourth, very few teams can lob well enough from the baseline to drive their opponents away from the net and set up winning points. Not even the pros can lob deep three times in a row.

Now don't misunderstand me here. If you're fairly new to the game, you may be wondering, "If playing the net is so important, why can't we just set up a tent at the net — just run up there and play?" Well, the problem is, you need to have weapons in order to attack; you have to earn your way up there with deep serves, accurate service returns, and strong volleys. If you lack these strokes but still come running forward, good teams will simply lob over your head or attack your weak side.

Also, playing aggressive doubles with a "storm the barrier, take over the fortress" attitude requires conditioning and a work ethic you may not be willing — or prepared — to undertake. And you may currently lack the strokes necessary to execute this strategy. Quite realistically you may be thinking, "Vic's telling us to serve and attack, volley, play the net, run back for lobs — but I can't do all that stuff. I'm just happy to be alive out there."

I'll admit, playing doubles like this means that you're constantly on the move — moving in behind your serve, breaking forward on a diagonal to cover volleys and drives, and retreating for lobs. You may be unprepared for the challenge, especially if you can beat your best serve to the net and volleying is a notable weakness and you're not in good enough shape to play this way for two sets and survive. And I'm also sympathetic to the fact that as some people grow older, they just don't have the speed, agility, and confidence to attack the net and roam that area once they get there. In this case, they should indeed stay back and work on their lobs. But there are also a lot of savvy players in their seventies and eighties still at the net who are wise about when to go and when to stay back.

If you're on the fence about all this, I'd suggest that you incorporate this aggressive approach gradually into your overall strategy. Serve and attack every other serve, or just once a set, and you'll have plenty of time to recover during crossovers. Moreover, this changing style could throw off your opponents by forcing them to return serve with greater precision as you rush the net. Remember, too, that you don't need a killer serve to come to the net; just keep it deep and you'll see how effective you can be.

If you're still thinking, "Thanks anyway, but I'd rather just stay back and try to win from the baseline," this is no problem — *if* you compete against opponents who also prefer to camp at the baseline or who play that universal system where one player is up near the net and the other is back deep. In fact, at the intermediate level, gaining the net is not as crucial as in 4.5/5.0-rated tennis; the team that gets there first often still loses the point because they tend to have weak volleys, they're more vulnerable to good lobs, and they frequently dump overheads into the net. Beginners find themselves in even more trouble; they usually rush up there in order to lose at a

9 The player at the net, playing aggressively, goes for a putaway overhead down the middle between two opponents caught deep.

faster rate, but I still encourage them to attack, since this is eventually how they should want to play the better they become.

You can stay back and try to win from a deep position, but this system cannot succeed against strong, aggressive teams. On a club ladder, for example, you may have good success against opponents who play the same defensive style and new teams that are just learning the game. But once these newcomers learn how to move to the net, they pass the teams that can only play defensively. So your team reaches a certain level, depending upon your ability to keep hard-charging teams pinned to the baseline with well-placed lobs and under constant pressure when they're up at the net with strong overheads and ground strokes from behind the baseline. But eventually your progress levels off.

If you want your team to keep moving up in class at the club or in your league, you must work on the shots, the movement skills, and mental attitude that will enable the two of you to play more aggressively. And, indeed, if you and your partner have short fuses and hate extended rallies, you have only one choice psychologically: Learn to attack the net. Instead of trying to dig in and win from the baseline, you must think aggressively and be ready to move forward at every opportunity.

What happens when your partner

refuses to play up at the net like this? You're going to have a new look, pal. Every time he stays back and leaves you at the net, a smart team is going to shell your right hip (where it's virtually impossible to get a racket on the ball), unless you turn your back as a sign of submission. If you stand up there against their overheads and try to fake them out, then you must take what they give you.

If you're miserable playing this way, simply find a new teammate. If dumping your partner is politically incorrect ("Vic, he's my husband!"), then help him improve his volley and his mental perception of how doubles ought to be played. Failing that, you must learn to capitalize on your net position by poaching, or crossing over early to the server's side to volley the anticipated return, not only on the serve but throughout every rally (see page 99).

2. Think about doubles as "10-second tennis." A second major emphasis in doubles should be the fact that time is at a premium. In topflight doubles everywhere, most points end so quickly — after the serve, a ground stroke return, one or two volleys, or an overhead, at most — that eventually you should visualize yourself playing little bursts of 10-second tennis. One consistency about doubles is that you have 8 to 12 seconds of excitement and then you go at it again, one roller coaster ride after another.

Still, I have to fight the image that persists at clubs around the world, where "one up, one back" doubles still prevails (see photo 10). Under this system, two players are deep — usually the server and the receiver — intently hitting the ball back and forth while trying to keep it away from the two players at the net. They're basically playing singles while their partners, glued to their ready positions, look over their shoulders and offer encouragement — "Hang in there, Bertha!" The only thing these net persons get is a stiff neck and a suntan on one side of their face; if a shot suddenly comes their way, they invariably dump it into the net — "Oh, I wasn't expecting that one" — because they're unprepared.

Unfortunately, as we'll see, leisurely "one up, one back" doubles is fun only if the other team promises to play along. Instead of falling into that trap, what counts is for you and your partner to appreciate just how little time and opportunity there is for each player to be a hero or a bum during each point. This will focus you on reality, not on the fantasy that you have the luxury of lengthy rallies in which to produce a winning shot or overcome a poor shot. It's not realistic to think, after the ball crosses the net two or three times, "I'll just get this shot back and keep the ball in play and we'll eventually win this thing," on about the tenth or twelfth shot.

Played right, a typical doubles point should develop like this: One person serves and rushes the net as the receiver tries to return the ball at his feet. Depending upon the success of this return shot, the server now either has an opportunity to volley a winner from above net level or must bend down to execute a low volley or half-volley — a defensive shot that raises the ball and allows his opponents to move in for a winning volley (as photos 12 A–D show).

All this happens fast, and the implications and demands are clear: Since the best teams in good doubles usually end the point by the third or fourth hit (it's even

10 When both teams play a "one up, one back" system, the point is often won by the baseline player with the soundest ground strokes. Notice that both net players are still primed for a volley opportunity, even when the ball keeps going back and forth between the baseline players.

11 The team in the foreground is trying to play "one up, one back" against a team that knows how to play (both players charging the net together at every opportunity). Player 2 is in deep trouble unless his partner can hit a great lob or a topspin drive just over the net.

12 A–D Using photos from different setups, we show how in a well-played point by the team returning serve, player 1 serves to the opponent's backhand (A). Player 2 returns the ball crosscourt, away from the net person and at the feet of the onrushing server (B). The service returner also follows his shot to the net (C), where he's now in a position to end the point with a putaway volley (D).

unusual for intermediate teams to average as many as five shots per rally, unless "keep it in play" opponents are involved), the stroking emphasis in doubles should be on the serve, the service return, and the volley — trailed by the lob, the overhead, and baseline ground strokes.

Furthermore, since the ball will seldom cross the net more than two or three times in a typical rally, take good care of the first shot that comes to you, because statistically it's your last. While this reminder may heighten the pressure you feel on each shot that you hit, it should also help improve

13 Whenever an opponent is bending down to hit a ball from below net level, you and your partner should attack. Here, the player in the foreground has his racket up and is anticipating a shot to his forehand. He's probably correct, since most half-volleys like this come down the center, but it's best to move forward holding the racket in a position that facilitates making either a forehand or backhand volley.

your concentration and the focus you bring to each stroke.

3. Always look for situations and try to create situations where your opponents are hitting up — and you can hit down. By and large, after the service return, your team should strive to keep the ball low and in the center of the court, while trying to take command of the net before your opponents do. When you can force your opponents to volley or half-volley from below net level, this puts them on the defensive and frees you to close in on the net, anticipating a return shot that will allow you to hit down. Neither of you has to be a world-beater to hit winning volleys and overheads from this vantage point.

Indeed, one of the most important things to realize about volleying in doubles is that the closer you can approach the net to volley, the less talent you need to win the point. And the farther back you are, the more talent is required. Most players think, "I don't have much talent, so I have to stay back," when actually just the reverse is true. Up near the net, you can volley at a

14 A–C The closer a team gets to the net to volley, the greater its chances of hitting a putaway. Notice how the angle widens for an aggressive volley as the two players in the foreground volley from the service line (A), two steps further in (B), and right on top of the net, another two steps closer (C).

A

B

C

130-degree angle just holding the racket in front of your face. But move back 12 or 15 feet to the service line area and there's only a 30-degree hitting angle, plus you need better technique and more strength to nail a volley.

Meanwhile, your team can't get pushed around by opponents who are continually having to lift the ball as they try to advance on the net. Few players in the history of the game have been able to take a low ball and convert it into an offensive volley with any real success.

4. Know your role — individually and as part of a team. When you're on the serving team, this should be your basic thrust: Get to the net . . . attack, attack, attack! You and your partner should be striving to keep the ball in play — away from the net person — and then looking for the first opportunity to end the point with a volley or an overhead, angling the shot away from the opposing team or placing it deep and down the middle.

When you're returning serve, your team should strive to seize the net away from the serving team (1) by hitting a strong return

15 The player closer to the net always has priority on the volley, even if it means invading his partner's territory.

at the feet of the onrushing server and moving in, since a low ball will force him to bend low and prevent him from hitting an aggressive shot, (2) by lobbing, if your opponents control the net (but only if it's deep!), or (3) by exploiting any lack of teamwork by your opponents, whereby you hit to an open part of the court.

Later in the book I'll talk about the fact that when your team attacks, your opponents may lob, so this demands that you and your partner know how to retreat quickly and how to retaliate with an overhead.

5. Court hogs spoil the fun — and lessen a team's potential success. There's a fine line between the properly aggressive player and the court hog. Basically, both players on a team should have the freedom to go for the ball, based on a fundamental principle: The player closer to the net has priority on the volley. Thus, if you have position on your partner — and the appropriate quickness — never be afraid to jump right in front and take the volley. Don't be scared off by "What are you doing on my side of the court?" That's a losing syndrome. What he's really saying is, "Look, partner, the closer you come to my side, the more our chances of losing increase." Instead of being intimidated, you must crowd the net, react quickly, and feel free to cross the center stripe for shots where you have the priority.

When you are working hard to protect

the team by trying to take every appropriate shot down the middle, nobody can accuse you of being a court hog. But you stand guilty when you try to go for every ball even though you're too slow or out of position and you proceed to disrupt your partner's shot. Or, equally destructive, she begins to think, "My partner will get it." The charge against the court hog on any team is that she creates indecision; immediately, only one player knows what's going to happen and the other has no clue or is reluctant to move, and this leads to chaos because there's no known pattern to their play against balls that are between them. The player without a clue becomes anxious, hesitant, afraid to trust her instincts. So she passes up balls she should be volleying, forcing her partner, willingly or not, to make the play, often in disadvantageous positions.

6. Focus on three shots: the serve, the service return, and the volley. If your team is pursuing an aggressive approach to doubles by trying to win at the net rather than from the baseline, the two of you should concentrate on practicing the serve, service return, and volley. These are the shots you'll be hitting repeatedly during a match, no matter which of the four positions you're playing at the start of any given point. Doubles needn't be much more complex than that. If you and your partner are comparatively strong at just two of the three shots mentioned above, the match is basically over, because your team will get those shots again and again.

7. Have automatic shot-making decisions in mind. I've found over the years that the mind should be more programmed in doubles than in singles.

A

B

16 A–B Sometimes baseline players hit too low and hard and don't give themselves time to get to the net. When you're certain your net-playing opponent won't poach, and his partner is way back, hit a higher ball back (A), which will give you more time to reach the net and make your opponent's return shot more difficult (B). Notice how the attacking team suddenly owns the net while the opponent is confronted by a high bouncer that's difficult to hit.

A

B

C

17 A–C Two net players will always try to keep the same distance between them, so that they don't get spread out and leave an easy target down the middle (A). Moving to the right, they keep the center closed to traffic (B), and moving to the left, it's just too tough to get past them with a shot (C).

There's so little time between shots (with two extra players on the court, the ball isn't traveling as far between hits) and there's the constant confusion posed by playing against two opponents (while also trying to play in harmony with a partner) that you should simplify your approach and reduce the variables you must confront in your mind.

The best doubles players enter a match with a series of automatic decisions and responses already programmed so that they can play with purposeful behavior but minimal conscious decision making. Playing instinctively like this is tough to do unless you and your partner determine, through experience, what each of you should try to do with specific shots in specific situations. Here are some of those prior decisions to make before going into a match:

- Always move toward the net whenever the ball goes deep in your opponents' court. Force them either to thread the needle with a passing shot between you or to hit a difficult lob over your heads.

- Lob if you're in trouble anywhere deep, especially if your opponents have taken the net.

- When your opponents are at the net, keep the ball low and down the middle as much as possible.

- Move in tandem with your partner — left, right, forward, and back, about 10 to 12 feet apart (see photos 17 A–C).

- If your team controls the net and your opponent tries to lob, you and your partner should turn and take three quick steps toward the baseline. Three steps will get you into good position for 90 percent of all lobs.

- Always anticipate and cover shots with an ultimate intention to gain control of the net.

Keeping these various principles in mind when you go to play, you can now explore how to maximize your chances of hooking up with a partner who's compatible with you for competitive doubles, both in tennis skills *and* personality.

CHAPTER 2

Choosing the Right Partner

LOOKING beyond the club's upcoming "Doubles and Dogs" barbecue event, when you have the time and opportunity to select an ongoing doubles partner, the extra effort is well worth it. Work it through carefully, because you could be picking a compatriot for years to come if you're fortunate. I know many people in clubs everywhere (and now also leagues) who have been partners for 10, 20, even 30 years, and they all say the same thing: When you have a good partner, you're just dying to play doubles all the time.

Taking a long-term perspective should encourage you to find a partner who is compatible not only as a player, but as a person you can enjoy playing with, whether you win or lose. While winning a club tournament — or Wimbledon — might be your ultimate goal, playing hard with a teammate and enjoying the competition and camaraderie should have priority. In fact, I'd prefer being paired with a winning *person* first and then worry about specific tennis skills, because congeniality is what wears best from match to match. I can understand why you might be willing to tolerate a partner's occasional on-court tantrums in exchange for his or her killer backhand, but over the long haul, through various ups and downs as a team, personal enjoyment and compatibility are what keep most partnerships together.

One good way to evaluate a prospective partner is simply to watch that person play with other people. You'll have little trouble assessing the person because a tennis match usually surfaces true personality traits. Then poke around and ask a few questions. Be wary, for example, of people who seem to have a compatibility shortcoming, moving from one partner to the next (though this is certainly not always the case, as evidenced by my compatible friend Jack Kramer, who won five Grand Slam tournaments with four different partners). If a gadfly partner still seems intriguing, try to talk with the player's former partners and check with the pro shop operator and certainly the league president, who invariably knows all the strengths and shortcomings of various players. Later in this chapter I'll suggest how you can utilize Jonathan Niednagel's Brain Typing expertise as you seek out and evaluate the right partner for your personality and playing style.

Matching Relative Playing Strengths and Weaknesses

"Matchup" is the key word as you try to find a partner who can mesh effectively with your preferred style of play *and* your personality.

Let's first look at stroking matchups.

Ideally, try to pair up with a player who has strengths that can help compensate for your specific shortcomings but also weaknesses that you can cover with your own particular skills. The two of you — individually and as a team — don't need every shot in the singles book in order to play good doubles, as long as your respective skills complement each other and you can call upon each other's strengths just at the right time.

You must also consider how your respective playing characteristics would mesh as a team, since certain combinations of strengths and weaknesses can prove disastrous in terms of winning matches against equally rated opponents.

For example, if the two of you are strong at the same strokes and weak at the same strokes, you will tend to lose against a better-balanced team, because your specific weaknesses will prove too exploitable. There's no hiding these vulnerable areas when you're up against a smart team.

More specifically, let's say that when your partner is receiving serve, you love to crowd the net and volley aggressively. This means you are totally dependent upon her ability to return the ball (1) away from the net player and (2) consistently at or near the feet of the onrushing server, which forces the server to hit up and allows you to attack and win points with your volley or overhead. If, instead, your partner continually returns the ball high and within easy range of the net player, this sets up putaway volleys for your opponents and wastes your particular strength, while spoiling your competitive enjoyment. Better to at least lose with a player who may have other weaknesses, but at least has a good service return that allows you to have fun playing the net.

Here's another consideration to keep in mind. Let's presume that your partner can indeed return serves at the feet of the onrushing server and loves to move in, but you hate to play the net, preferring instead to fall back and play from the baseline. Here, your partner's doubles strength is negated by your particular weakness, which in this scenario allows the opposing team to escape the challenge of a strong service return while it takes uncontested control of the net.

Choosing a partner, therefore, requires understanding the roles of all four players in doubles (see chap. 5) as you seek somebody who can help you create a winning team. Then use the following checklist to gather further ideas about stroking matchups.

18 The goal of player 2 is to return the serve crosscourt, away from the net player and at the feet of the onrushing server. This forces the server to hit up and allows the receiving team to move confidently up to the net, ready to volley or to hit an overhead. Player 2 should advance along the dotted line in order to narrow the gap between himself and his partner; the server then has to hit a difficult crosscourt shot to get the ball past player 2 on the left.

19 Against the serve, if your partner returns the ball high and within range of an aggressive net player, that player will continually nail you up at the net.

A Partner Checklist

- Make sure your prospective partner is not intent on playing the side you want to play (i.e., the right side "deuce" court or the left side "ad" court), unless you are prepared to compromise. Most players already know the side they prefer (though it may not necessarily be their *best* side) and will voice their disapproval at having to play an unfamiliar side or will simply play poorly on this side. When players develop a motor program for a particular side, switching opens up a whole new world for them and is usually a losing proposition in the short run. Nevertheless, once you have played several matches with a new partner (and even as you assess your own current partnership in light of the advice I give in this book), don't be afraid to experiment by changing sides. Many players never realize that their strength is in playing the opposite of their usual side until forced to do so by a new partnership — when they lose a coin toss or the dominant personality gets his or her choice. Also, teammates occasionally switch positions to break up a losing pattern, or when one player thinks he could be better on the other side and asks his partner to switch.

Pro opponents keep a book on strengths and weaknesses of opponents from a particular position, but that book goes out the window the first time they switch sides. Before permanently teaming up in 1992, Gigi Fernandez and Natasha Zvereva had played before together "and it wasn't great," said Fernandez. "I think that's because Natalia was playing the backhand and I was playing the forehand at the time. This time, I told her we should try it the other way around — that I should play the ad court and she should play the deuce court." After that, the Grand Slam titles began falling into place.

- If you're a right-hander and you enjoy playing the left side, you may want a left-hander, so that your team has two forehands down the middle. Also, the left-hander may like the right side if he has a "flat," underspin backhand service return, because his natural swing produces a shot that travels away from the net player.
- Perhaps you're a flashy player who loves to take chances but you play erratically and you realize the need for an even-keel partner who is steady and reliable.
- If you're slow afoot, better make sure you find someone who's fast, or at least quicker than you are. Two plodders, even with good volleying skills, are rarely going to win many events.
- Height can also be a factor. If you're relatively short, a taller partner can help compensate, especially if you can contribute greater foot speed to the team. When Lisa Raymond (5'5") and upcoming singles star Lindsay Davenport (6'2") formed a partnership in 1994 (and beat Fernandez and Zvereva, the best women's team in the world, in only their fourth tournament together), Raymond noted: "Lindsay can cover more of the higher balls, and she's got the wingspan that I don't have. I've got the wheels, so to speak. I'm more mobile and closer to the ground."
- If you enjoy playing the net, concentrate on finding a person who can return the serve low over the net and, ideally, near the feet of the onrushing server. This will give you a chance to win many points with volleys and overheads on the third shot of the rally.

In fact, if I personally had to pick a partner who had only one particular

20 When a right-hander has a left-handed partner, the lefty will often play the right side so that the team has two forehand volleys and overheads down the middle.

strength, and all his other strokes were mediocre, I would emphasize the service return. That specific skill would keep us in the match by always providing us the potential to break serve, because I would be up at the net, capitalizing on my quickness (yes, quickness!), good anticipation, and a strong volley. Then on my serve I'd be coming in and joining my partner at the net, where doubles is decided. (Back in high school, in Monroe, Michigan, I won a lot of tournaments with partners who weren't as fast as I was and were happy to accept their role: Keep the ball in play, either deep or short, and give Braden a chance to poach. It was a nice balance. My partners took their responsibility quite seriously and I loved to poach; that was the real fun in doubles for me. Later in life, in my first pro tournament, I almost won a set against Bobby Riggs, chasing everything down until I finally wore down and lost the match. For some reason, Bobby still remembered that match we played in the Cleveland Arena 40 years later and would tell people whenever we were together, "That little Braden was really fast.")

Personality Matchups

Searching for the "right" long-term partner also asks for some important soul-searching

21 Count your blessings when you have a partner who can return serve by aggressively moving forward into the ball and driving it away from the net player, on both his forehand and backhand sides.

on your part, in terms of being honest with yourself about just who you ought to play with from a psychological and competitive point of view. While your tennis-playing skills might mesh well with a prospective partner, does he or she share your approach to the game? How about personal compatibility and personality factors such as egos, competitive spirit, emotional control, and almost everybody's need for positive reinforcement?

Where you place the emphasis here will depend on your priorities. Ask yourself these two critical questions: (1) Is your main goal to play competitively yet have fun with a person you enjoy, on and off the court? or (2) Do you have a narrower focus, in which winning a giant trophy — or a league championship — is what counts, even if it means accepting a partner who's difficult to abide at times? If winning indeed takes precedence, then you may have to sacrifice some enjoyment while suffering certain aspects of your partner's personality.

The Competitive-Spirit Issue

If you haven't yet made up your mind about a prospective partner, it is very important to assess just how competitive she is when it comes to doubles. If you're an aggressive person who really wants to win but you're contemplating playing with a person who — at least on the surface — doesn't seem to worry that much about the final outcome, then you possibly should avoid a partnership. Nor should you pair up with a "winning is everything" type of player if other things about doubles are more important to you.

The key is psychological synchronization. Below are some questions to ask a prospective partner as a way to anticipate just how well your personalities and expectations will match up. Sit down with the person (whom you likely already know as a friend, a relative, or somebody you've watched play at the club) and have a conversation in the spirit of, "Here's who I am, how about you?" Since we don't always evaluate ourselves accurately and objectively, this is not a sure way to determine compatibility, but it's a start. (This list of questions should also be raised with people who have played with your prospective partner.)

- Just how important is winning to you? What are your expectations in case we team up? If you can't abide losing and you want to win every match but you're playing with someone who doesn't appear to have his heart in the competition, then you're going to find yourself too frustrated too often.
- How consistent is your competitiveness? Do you like to work hard? Most of us enjoy playing with people who try to give it their all, win or lose, throughout the match. So try to screen out early the person who starts to lose interest as the team falls behind or who sometimes wants to play hard but at other times makes it clear he would rather be doing something else.
- When you are losing, how do you feel? Even if you are personally playing well, how do you tend to react? One reason you should be seeking a partner who can talk honestly to you is that you don't want to be surprised — or shocked — by his behavior. There are enough emotional surprises in the course of a normal match.
- When you're playing poorly in a particular match, how do you usually respond? Are you outwardly emotional? Or do you keep it bottled up? Honesty is appreciated here because some players suppress their true competitiveness until they make a particularly grievous error and then suddenly erupt like a wild person, which can certainly be unsettling and embarrassing.
- How do you want your partner to act toward you when you're not playing well, or when you miss a key shot or blow an easy overhead? Do you prefer pep talks or the silent treatment? How do you tend to treat your partner in similar circumstances? Do you get exasperated? Or can you shake it off? In stressful, competitive circumstances, I think everybody treasures the partner who understands that you're trying your best and that you don't need to be reminded that you're playing poorly. A partner's job is to provide some time for the struggling player to regain his confidence by poaching and trying to cover more court. A relaxed player has a better chance of recovering his game when his partner lets him know in some way, "Hey, we've been in this situation before and we've pulled it out," and he finds something to laugh about. This certainly isn't accomplished with subtle reminders of his lousy play.

If you can raise questions like these and communicate up front with your eventual partner, then your doubles relationship is going to be more comfortable and rewarding for both of you. By understanding each other like this from the beginning and by being realistic about what you're getting into, you'll minimize the potential misunderstandings and surprises that can eventually erode and sabotage the partnership.

Searching out a harmonious partner doesn't always mean the two of you need to have similar personalities. In fact, I've watched some great teams over the years that are psychologically and emotionally sound for no apparent reason. One player is boisterous, the other calm and collected, yet they understand each other and benefit from that synergy, where one person is the calming agent at turbulent moments in the match while the other pokes the coals when the team needs a lift.

Where Brain Typing Can Help

In the introduction, I mentioned Jonathan Niednagel, an expert at identifying specific personality types and accompanying motor skills through Brain Typing. According to Niednagel, "This personality evaluation technique is going to help people choose a tennis partner who is compatible and it's going to help people identify and understand the person who is not compatible." He notes that once people have a fundamental understanding of Brain Typing (e.g., one aspect being left-brain versus right-brain dominance), they can choose many different brain types as partners, but for different reasons.

For example, if relationships mean more to you than winning or losing, then you should choose a friendly partner, so the two of you can laugh your heads off when you play. You may not win many matches (but then again you may), but you go for it and you have a great time. The high-energy, friendly, and organized "EFJ" type is strong on relationships, maintaining harmony, and getting along with people. A lot of women who run tennis leagues and tennis clubs are like this and they often find themselves burned out after about six months by all the infighting and their efforts to keep the peace among the many little factions that always seem to exist.

Says Niednagel,

> We know there are 8 "thinking" brain types and 8 "feeling" brain types out of the 16 that Jung identified (and we may identify 32 as we get more sophisticated with our testing and observations). Feeling types are much more apt to be harmonious; they may get competitive, but when it's over they are usually not going to be mad or carry a grudge. In doubles, this type of person might want to pick a partner who has been identified as a right-brain feeling type, since this person is usually more risk-taking and athletic than a left-brain feeling type. Or, you could pick a feeling type who may get a little emotional during a match but is still there to encourage you overall and be happy afterwards. There's a happy median here — you can still win with a feeling type.

Taking the 16 identified brain types, Niednagel places them in four groupings:

> One group specializes in *tactical awareness*. They are continually thinking about what's going on right now in play and "How can I jump on that and take advantage of that person's weakness instantly?"

This kind of player, of course, is great to have as a doubles partner.

A second group is more into *strategies*. When these individuals are on a team that loses, they think about that loss afterwards, dissecting everything that went wrong, trying to figure out just how the other team had used better strategy and tactics to beat them. And then they try to come up with a strategy to counterattack that strategy the next time the two teams meet.

Group three loves *logistics*. These players basically work so hard, trying to get everything down just right — the stroking fundamentals, every little mechanical function — that this is primarily what they think about, and very often they let strategy and tactics slide. In fact, they may have a perfect stroke but they don't do anything about their moves and they lose.

And the fourth group is much more into *relationships* and *personal harmony;* they're thinking first and foremost about liking what they're doing and playing with people that they like. So they hate to play certain people and will become highly agitated before certain matches because of the people they are playing.

Niednagel emphasizes that everybody has all these abilities in some sense but are much stronger in certain areas than in others.

When you understand these groupings, you can more easily realize that if you're a certain type, you may need a tactician as your doubles partner in order to keep your team in the match because you personally can't think tactically as you play. You have trouble just keeping track of the score.

Another interesting combination that comes up in doubles but can be prevented by an awareness of Brain Typing is the team in which one partner loves to strategize everything but his partner says, "Don't fill me with all that junk; I just want to hit the ball." They are always in conflict because one player is reading books and studying videos while the other person just wants to go with the flow. Obviously they are mismatched brain types.

Taking a cue from Niednagel, here's another example to consider as you seek a partner. There are people who simply don't like being pushed into making quick decisions, which means they are missing a primary mental requisite for doubles. Introverted, left-brain persons who like to gather data and spend a good deal of time digesting this data are not your optimal doubles players and perform better in singles, especially on slower clay courts. For those of you who can personally identify with these cautious tendencies, playing doubles with a nonjudgmental partner can be of great benefit. Doubles play will force you to become a faster decision-maker while improving your volleying skills.

In a similar sense, certain brain types are risk-takers; they have excellent fine-motor skills and they love to go to the net, but they inadvertently choose a doubles partner who won't go to the net, who hates playing up there. This again leads to giant arguments. The aggressive player knows the team must play up at the net — together — as often as possible in order to win; this person knows that a player close to the net can volley at about a 130-degree angle, whereas the player who hangs back and volleys from around the service line has only about a 30-degree hitting angle away from the opponents and must be a more skilled volleyer. The odds eventually win out for the team that is volleying more often from near the net, as opposed to the team that lies back. So, obviously, you should try to play with a person who is aggressive, who can get to the net and gain that volleying angle away from the opposing team. Conversely, you should avoid the player who elects to stay at the baseline and is unwilling to change.

Much of this has to do with a person's psychological makeup. Niednagel's data show that some people won't go to the net because they lack the risk-taking factor, and this is because they think in the conservative part of their brain, in the rear of the left side. "For them to even *think* about going to the net is crazy talk," he says. "So if your partner is a talented player who can move but refuses to venture up, it may be that the sense of security that he gets by staying back is greater than his sense of adventure and his desire to win."

As Niednagel emphasizes, "The thing always to remember about brain types is that even though the advice makes sense (e.g., get to the net at every opportunity!), some players simply don't care because they have fixed, rigid personalities. So if you have a brain type that predisposes you to taking action and playing aggressively, avoid the pain of playing with a person who simply doesn't want to play this style of doubles."

He adds, however, that "if they can learn to get along with one another, opposite types can be ideal tennis partners. For example, a high-energy, organized person can be complemented by a less-energized (particularly off the court), adaptable partner. Both of their mental and physical skills can assist the team, much like Pam Shriver and Martina Navratilova once demonstrated."

Husband-and-Wife Pairings

My colleague Bud Collins once said, "Talk to any marriage counselor and you'll learn that mixed doubles has caused more divorces than mothers-in-law." But I love it when husbands and wives want to play together, provided they've clearly communicated *why* they've decided to pair up. In this situation, as in the other partnership-forming decisions I've discussed, the key is always communication — open and direct.

Here are some questions for you and your spouse to think about and ask each other before you commit to playing together as a serious, competitive team beyond those social and charitable events around town. Remember, even though you may be happily married, you are still two different people playing together out on the tennis court — whatever your motivations and rewards might be — and you bring along different sets of competitive goals and values. This is where trouble often arises if you fail to discuss these potentially divisive issues ahead of time and, indeed, throughout your partnership.

1. Do you feel you have the ability to say no to this partnership before it even begins? Will you be able to call it off if you sense at any point that playing together is actually proving detrimental to your marriage?
2. When you play together, what

bothers you the most about your spouse's behavior? When does his or her behavior distract you from the tennis?
3. When you make an error and are playing poorly, what body language does your spouse project that drives you nuts?
4. What's the fun part of playing together?
5. How often should you try to play together? When are you going to practice?

Meanwhile, take into account the possibility that one married partner *has* to win but the other doesn't care that much either way. Or that one player hates to practice and would rather play singles between matches, while the other loves to practice, knowing that if you want to play good doubles and you want to win, you have to practice. There are also the social aspects to consider, where, for example, the husband may want to hang around the club and be really involved, while his wife just wants to play their match and beat a hasty retreat home.

It's important to hash these things out so that doubles can help the marriage prosper. In fact, the answers to your questions may surprise you and could reveal reasons why you and your spouse should never play together or may actually help bring a better understanding to the partnership. Otherwise, what often develops is that the husband tries to make the woman play the way that he wants her to play and conform to his set of rules. And it doesn't simply mean encouraging her to stay in the alleys as he tries to cover the rest of the court. The problem is that he can't understand why his wife is not as excited about their doubles team as he is, not as excited about practicing, not as excited rehashing the match they've just played. And, of course, it also goes the other way with women who love the competition and the whole tennis scene but have complacent husbands when it comes to hard-nosed tennis talk.

Either way, if you're playing basically in order to please your spouse, this can lead to trouble by adding underlying tension to the partnership, unless the two of you have a healthy outlook on why you are playing together. Another dangerous aspect about husband-wife teams is that people will say hurtful things to people they love, disparaging remarks that they would never say to other people out on the tennis court. Just be aware that this is a trait that can surface under the pressure of playing a competitive sport together in a stressful situation.

Ultimately, try to realize that you don't have to play tennis together as an affirmation that you have a happy marriage. Even if it's a fund-raising event for Aunt Ethel's favorite charity, if you don't want to play with your spouse, say so. Why spoil the fun for yourself and a lot of other players?

Preparing for the End of the Partnership at the Beginning

This may sound coldhearted, but since most doubles teams fail to hang together for more than a couple of years, you and your partner should bring up the worst-case scenario right at the beginning: how eventually to end the relationship, short of death, divorce, injury, or an out-of-town move. An early discussion along these lines with your partner, before you've ever played together, will give both of you a more graceful, accessible way to part company when one of you is unhappy with the situation — even if this dissatisfaction surfaces after just one or two matches together.

We all know how hard it can be to open up a conversation of this nature, but it's much easier — and you'll minimize hurt feelings — when you've at least discussed the possibility at the beginning of the merger. Just simply talk with your partner and say, "This looks like it's going to be a great partnership, but what if it doesn't work out?" The two of you should decide what an unhappy partner ought to do, so that both of you will always have a comfortable system to follow and there are no hurtful surprises, such as hearing from a third person that your partner is terminating the partnership. "All's fair in love, war and doubles partners," said Pam Shriver, who learned over the phone that Martina Navratilova was ending their long partnership, "but there should be an etiquette for splitting up. You shouldn't do it by phone, you shouldn't do it by letter. You should do it in person."

With the separation issue settled early and before the first ball has gone between you as you both cry "Yours!" it's actually time to play a match together.

CHAPTER 3

Early Teamwork Decisions and Preparations

ONCE you have a partner, the two of you should resolve a number of key questions before actually stepping on the court to play as a team.

1. Is Your Team Going to Have a Captain?

While the "team captain" concept sounds great (in keeping with the American tradition of always having a boss for any group of two or more people), my experience has been that it limits a team's potential. The problem that occurs when one person takes control (often without a word ever being said) is that the other person feels dependent and very often will not make a decision that's in the best interest of the team — for example, waiting too long to move and take a shot he should be hitting. Instead, he's continually saying "Yours!"

Still, every doubles team must resolve the question, subtle as it might be: Who calls the shots on the team and who actually dictates strategy and court-coverage decisions?

I prefer to see teams in which, instead of thinking that one person should take control as the on-the-court captain, each player assumes responsibility for being a leader in his or her own way. This means splitting the "leadership" 50-50, so that each player senses the challenge — and freedom — to contribute his or her particular strengths to a team effort. This way, whatever your personality might be, you can play knowing that you have the freedom to make things happen.

For example, if you're a quiet player

with a rather submissive personality, you could easily be intimidated by a boisterous partner, despite your doubles skills. You need the ability to assert your tennis strengths and defer your weaknesses as you evolve a relationship with your partner.

When a team acknowledges that doubles should be a 50-50 responsibility, each player recognizes his role at the beginning of each match and then plays to his strengths and weaknesses while taking control of his 50 percent share, except when circumstances call for one player to step forward and assume greater responsibility for holding the team together.

Without a team captain, both of you are giving up the individual control of singles on behalf of the team, so compromises are crucial. Perhaps it will help to remember that, psychologically, everybody has a control system, and this "system" does not like to be controlled. One reason some people have difficulty adjusting to doubles after playing singles is that in singles they control all the variables on their side of the net, but in doubles they must contend with variables over which they lack complete control — namely, their partner's personality and playing ability. So there's a fear, and sometimes a frustration, of losing control. That's why I emphasize a 50-50 understanding, with partners sharing the "control," each person taking charge of his or her own game within the partnership, and trying not to go beyond those limits.

If you decide to have a captain, try to work out an understanding beforehand as to what this role actually involves and what the parameters are, so that you and your partner are not suddenly squabbling during the match, when you should be concentrating on your tennis.

2. Who Should Play Which Side of the Court?

Several important considerations will help determine which side of the court you and your partner should play (assuming here that both of you are right-handers). But start with this basic understanding: The weaker player, whether he or she plays the left or right side, at whatever level, is going to get most of the shots — until the other team realizes it is losing too many points with this strategy.

There's no hiding the more vulnerable player from an attacking team, although self-appointed "captains" try hard to do so. One example is the overzealous, misguided husband I described in the introduction who pairs up with a submissive wife who doesn't know better. He tries to assign her a playing cubicle in the doubles alley, right in front of the net, so that she's out of harm's way while he takes on the other team. But this "hide a partner" strategy rarely works. Assuming she doesn't have much of a role, the wife backs away from her playing responsibilities and is too intimidated to try for shots that are legitimately within her range. Meanwhile, her husband runs out of gas trying to chase down every ball.

If you find yourself in a pickup tournament at the club or a big charity event, and your assigned partner tries to pull this "strategy" on you, assert your basic rights as a doubles partner — and then prove yourself as a capable doubles player. Don't let your partner arbitrarily relegate you to the doubles alleys and intimidate you away from the ball, because that's not the way doubles is supposed to be played — or enjoyed. Doubles is an equal partnership.

22 On the backhand return from the deuce court, the hitter strives to keep his head down and contact the ball comfortably out in front of his body so that he can drive it crosscourt at the onrushing server, away from the net player. If the receiver lifts his head early, before contact, he'll usually pull the ball to the net player for an easy putaway.

With this in mind, consider the demands and the shots that go with each side of the court (assuming, again, that both partners are right-handed).

Ideally, the right-side player, on service returns, needs a strong crosscourt forehand and a strong crosscourt backhand in order to keep the ball away from the netman. This player should also have a reliable backhand volley from the middle of the court, once the point is under way.

On the left side, the player returning serve must also be able to hit a backhand crosscourt and a forehand crosscourt away from the netman. However, the ad court is more forgiving to the player with a weak backhand, since it accommodates the across-the-body swing that pulls the ball naturally crosscourt. The left-court player also needs a strong forehand volley against shots down the middle, especially if he has to compensate for a partner's weak backhand volley. Also, if there's a disparity in overhead abilities, the player with the stronger overhead should try to play the left court, so that he can comfortably "cheat" to his partner's side to take lobs to his forehand side.

I have always advocated having the weaker player on the right side, because it's easier for that person to run around the backhand to hit a forehand against the serve. (The server is limited as to where he can position himself along the baseline in order to hit the ball into the backhand corner of the deuce court. Serving from the left side to the ad court, he can stand near the sideline, if necessary, to keep pressure on the opponent's backhand.) The weaker backhand player will normally tell you he prefers the right court.

Personality factors are also important. If you're a flashy player who thrives on pressure and loves center stage, I think you should play the left side. For one thing, when you're receiving serve and you have the ad, you're now in a position to hit away with abandon, win the point, and break serve. And, if you're down the ad, it doesn't matter — you feel confident you can help get it back to deuce by hitting a strong return. Also, if you like to cut to the middle, playing the left side will give you a longer reach on your forehand side to poach an opponent's shot (as opposed to poaching from the right side with a backhand volley).

Meanwhile, in advanced tennis, the steady, conservative, more consistent player — a person who may lack flashy shots but hardly ever misses a service return — should play the right side. In fact, the great doubles teams in history have been made by a right-court player who can return serve. This is the pressure court — at 30-all and deuce — and if the receiver can get the serve back and help win the point here (e.g., by laying the ball at the feet of the onrushing server and setting up a putaway for her partner at the net), then all the pressure goes on the server to hold serve. The right-court player also tends to be a logical thinker who enjoys strategic ploys and crafty shots.

My friend Gene Mako, who teamed with

A

B

23 A–B From the ad court, the player who pulls across his backhand can often hit a perfect service return along the dotted line (A). But that same type of shot from the deuce court goes right to the net person for an easy volley (B).

Don Budge to win four Wimbledon and U.S. Open titles, was a great right-court player. Returning serve, he said his attitude was to "get that ball in play," so Budge (or other partners, such as Gardner Malloy) could close out the point with an aggressive volley. Mako also told me, "The first year I played with Budge, I played the left side because I was more experienced. But as it became obvious that he was the stronger player, and since he loved to roam and attack with his forehand volley, we decided to switch. My job was to help win the point on deuce so Don could then win the game with his great backhand return." Mako also said that while most teams settle on fixed court positions from one tournament to the next, one of his partners, Jack Tidball, preferred a more flexible approach. "At a tournament, Jack would come down to breakfast and tell me who was going to play which side that day. But we won a lot of tournaments together."

The Mixed-Doubles Myth

Another worldwide myth in mixed doubles is the prevailing belief that the woman ("weaker") should always play the right court, while the man ("stronger") should always play the left. This is a limiting presumption. Instead, the stronger overall player should play the left side, especially one who's a little flashier — and that could be the man *or* the woman. Perhaps the only way to find this out is to experiment, but that's one of the enjoyments of doubles, trying to determine your strongest links as a team.

Just remember, though: It's the right-court player who very likely will make your team famous, especially in mixed doubles. Believe me, more women have won a tournament for the man than the other way around. She's the key to the whole thing, for if she can volley aggressively, crowd the net, react quickly, and cross the center stripe for shots where she has priority, her team will put severe pressure on opponents. They will have to treat her team as a *team,* rather than intimidate her into inaction at the net while they run her partner into the ground. In team tennis competition around the country, directors will tell you that the teams with the most consistent woman win more often than the teams with the best man.

Think about it. When the woman's male partner is serving, his strong serve produces a weak return — and who's at the net to capitalize? The woman. Even if her volley is not that strong — just accurate — she can win the point outright, or at least put her opponents on the defensive. Then when she serves, the man is at the net, and if she has just a reasonably effective serve — consistently deep — she sets him up for a winning volley or overhead. Even if her serve is comparatively weak, the man can play aggressively from net post to net post, poach, take his shots, and help her hold serve. This is what produces a winning team.

When the husband arbitrarily puts his wife in the right court, regardless of their relative abilities, a "checks and balances" system fortunately exists that can help the woman get even at the end of a losing day. Remember, when she serves, her husband loves to poach at the net and he wins lots of points, which helps her hold serve. But when the husband serves, if the wife doesn't like to volley and is afraid to poach, her husband usually loses his serve to an aggressive team.

Now they're driving home and they start having a gigantic argument about who was to blame for their loss. But the wife flattens her husband immediately. "Don't look at me," she says. "I won every serve."

The Service-Return Factor

Looking at positioning from another perspective, on an evenly matched team I'd prefer to have the person with the most reliable service return play the right court, no matter if he's a righty or a lefty. Here's why.

When a game goes to 30-all or deuce, the player on the right side (who has a stronger return than his partner) now has a better chance than his partner to gain the advantage by hitting an effective return that puts their opponents on the defensive. If he does so, and his team wins the point, this takes pressure off his partner in the ad court by giving him a chance to help win the game just by getting the serve back in play. This left-court person can hit aggressively, knowing, "If I flub my return, no problem; the score goes back to deuce and my partner gets another opportunity to gain the ad."

When the player with a weaker service return plays the right court, the downside is that when the score reaches deuce, he often creates trouble by hitting a weak return that leads to a lost point. This puts all the pressure on his partner's subsequent return from the ad court. The best his partner can do is get the score back to deuce, which simply gives the right-court player a second chance to hit the right shot.

Still, it may be that even though you have a better return than your partner, playing the left side is preferable because you relish the challenge when the game is ad either way. Here you're in a position either to break serve with a strong return or to save your team by getting the score back to deuce, with an attitude of "I've got to hit a good one or we're out of here." Of course, you need a competitive spirit to want this kind of challenge, over and over again, and it's something that should be discussed with your partner beforehand. You should ask, "When we're receiving, would you rather play the right court — which means returns in the deuce situation — or the left court?"

Basically, try to find a Michael Jordan–type person to patrol the left court, a player who can hit hard and think aggressively and optimistically, whatever the score. You should be playing here if you're more likely than your partner to be thinking, when the ad is against you, "I can win the point and save us," or to be thinking, if you're up the ad, "I can win the game here." Just like the basketball player who demands the ball when his team is down by two points with six seconds left, the left-court player in doubles should have the confidence that he can handle the pressure when his team's fate is on the line.

3. What Side Should the Lefty Play?

At the inexperienced and intermediate level, where opponents try much more often to hit down alleys, left-handers are more effectively deployed on the left side if the partner is right-handed. This arrangement gives a team forehands down each alley.

Against experienced players, who strive

24 The worst doubles system in the world is "one up and one back" on both teams. It's called "singles doubles."

to hit down the middle of the court, the left-hander should try to play the right side (when teamed with a right-hander). This gives a team two forehands against "down the middle" shots. It also offers the lefty an advantage when hitting a backhand service return, since he can swing across his body — the natural tendency — and still pull the ball away from the netman, toward the feet of the onrushing server.

Nevertheless, any team that has a lefty should experiment with right-side and left-side alignments before fixing positions, since the lefty may lack a consistent return in the deuce court and may actually play better on the ad side.

4. What System of Play Will You Try to Emphasize?

The best "system" for doubles is to have both players of the same team at the net together, since most points will be won or lost at the net. The team with both players at the net, moving together, will almost always control the point against baseliners.

The second-best alignment is for both players to stay back at the baseline, trying to win from there with strong ground strokes, lobs, and retrieving ability.

The worst system — yet the one most universally played at the club level — has one player up at the net and the other

25 An aggressive team can be deadly when volleying from close to the net, especially against a team that has one player up and one player back.

player back (see photo 24). This is a system that can succeed only if the other team promises to play it too.

When both teams play "one up, one back," the two opposing players in the backcourt basically play singles, rallying back and forth, while the net players become frozen in their ready positions as they watch the ball travel from baseline to baseline. The players at the net are not going anywhere — it's not their turn to play — but invariably the ball comes to one of them and, startled, that person proceeds to dump it into the net.

While "one up, one back" doubles can be fun at a club where everybody else follows suit, the strategy falls apart against a team that knows how to play the game. If your team starts out playing one up and one back, savvy opponents will hit to your deep player, then immediately take the net. The player who is back now hits the ball toward the opponents, one of whom proceeds to nail the player who had the guts to stay at the net instead of retreating to the baseline.

Trying to play "one up, one back" against a team that comes to the net at every opportunity also creates enormous gaps in your defense, allowing your opponents to hit putaways all day long. And they can continue to drill their volleys and overheads at the poor person on your team who remains at the net, attempting to hold down the fortress.

The Australian Formation

I still see this alignment used occasionally, even on the pro tour, with both players on the serving team starting on the same side of the center stripe. Instead of serving and going straight forward, as you see in photo 26, the server moves in diagonally to cover a "down the line" return, while his partner closes in on the net.

The Australian is usually deployed by a team that's getting blown away and is trying to break the other team's rhythm and winning momentum, though it can also be used if one team is ahead but the opponents are suddenly on a hot streak. Specifically, if an opponent has been killing the serving team with her crosscourt returns, the Australian positions the partner of the server up at the net waiting to volley her favorite shot. If the receiver chooses to avoid that low-percentage challenge, she must "reprogram" her intended return, which can lead to hitting errors.

26 In the rarely used Australian Formation, both players on the serving team stand on the same side of the court to start the point.

5. What's the Best Ready Position?

Beginners always want to know the answer to this question, but I always have to tell them: There is no universal ready position. Rather, it's the most comfortable position from which you can break for the ball quickly and in control. Besides, you never hit a ball while in the ready position; it's all for show. That's why we all hate to play doubles with people who are enamored with their ready position, because they hate to leave home to volley. They're always saying, "Yours!" and you can spot them at the club from a mile away.

While indeed the top male and female players over the past 50 years have devised various ready positions, getting up on one's toes as the ball is being struck or just before impact is universally accepted as the best way to go. This prestretches the calf muscles and allows them to rebound faster.

6. Who Should Serve First?

Simple arithmetic dictates that the player with the best serve should serve first in doubles, since he (or she) has the chance of serving one more game than his partner in each set, as well as finishing off a tiebreaker. Still, there are circumstances that might dictate a different philosophy. Maybe the person who has the stronger serve needs two or three games to get sufficiently warmed up, mentally and physically. The wind and the sun are other factors to consider and should be discussed with your partner beforehand. When Pancho Gonzalez won the coin toss, he would occasionally let his opponent serve first in singles, just to get the person thinking, "I wonder why he's doing that?" But of course Pancho had such an indomitable serve, he could gamble a bit with his tactics.

If you're about to play a match, be happy if you hear someone on the other side ask, "Hey, should I serve first, or do you want to go first?" This means your opponents either haven't played together before (which usually poses a hurdle for teams to overcome) or haven't spent much time communicating with one another, which is a tip-off to teamwork shortcomings that your team can exploit.

When your team is serving first, make sure that both of you have warmed up as though you've already started the match. The reason for this is that the first serving game is often won by the return team because the server has not yet found his rhythm. Also, the receiver knows that his chances are much better in early games before the server is cranked up.

In fact, the psychology of a strong receiving team is to break the serving team the first time they serve — and then hang on. Since most servers tend to hold serve in tournament tennis, an early break can prove demoralizing. With this philosophy in mind, the strong receiving team will usually try to poach early to give the server something extra to worry about as he serves and goes to the net. Some teams will also lob early to test the overhead ability of the serving team. As with serves, overheads aren't practiced enough in the warm-up and often fail the hitter when the pressure is on in the early going.

Court Positions to Start a Point

GOOD doubles is organized chaos, a blur of four bodies moving up, back, and laterally, each person trying to react to shots instinctively or with premeditated decisions, and each team striving to gain the net, where quick reactions and aggressive volleying skills win out.

Moments before this swirling action begins, however, a lot of thinking and anticipation should be going on in the mind of each player as they prepare to play their roles from their respective court positions.

There are no special rules regarding positioning before the serve, except that the server cannot foot fault (as in singles) and both opponents must receive serve on alternating serves. You might think of this as the rule to protect against the Bobby Riggs of the sport. Paired up with former pro John Faunce, the consummate hustler once had a huge bet with two opponents. He felt pretty certain he could win if he could just play them by himself (Faunce was a stylish but more defensive player, and Bobby feared he would choke while playing for big money), so when he served and received serve, he had Faunce stand to the side (or even sit on the bench, as I heard in one version) as he took on the other team. Bobby even had Faunce serve and then get off the court, but he couldn't hide his partner when it was Faunce's turn to receive serve. Don't ask me to analyze why Faunce would enjoy a charade like this, but the money was good — and Riggs knew that by playing alone he actually put more pressure on his opponents.

Curious to know just how that match came out, I called Bobby's close friend Lornie Kuhle in October 1995. I knew

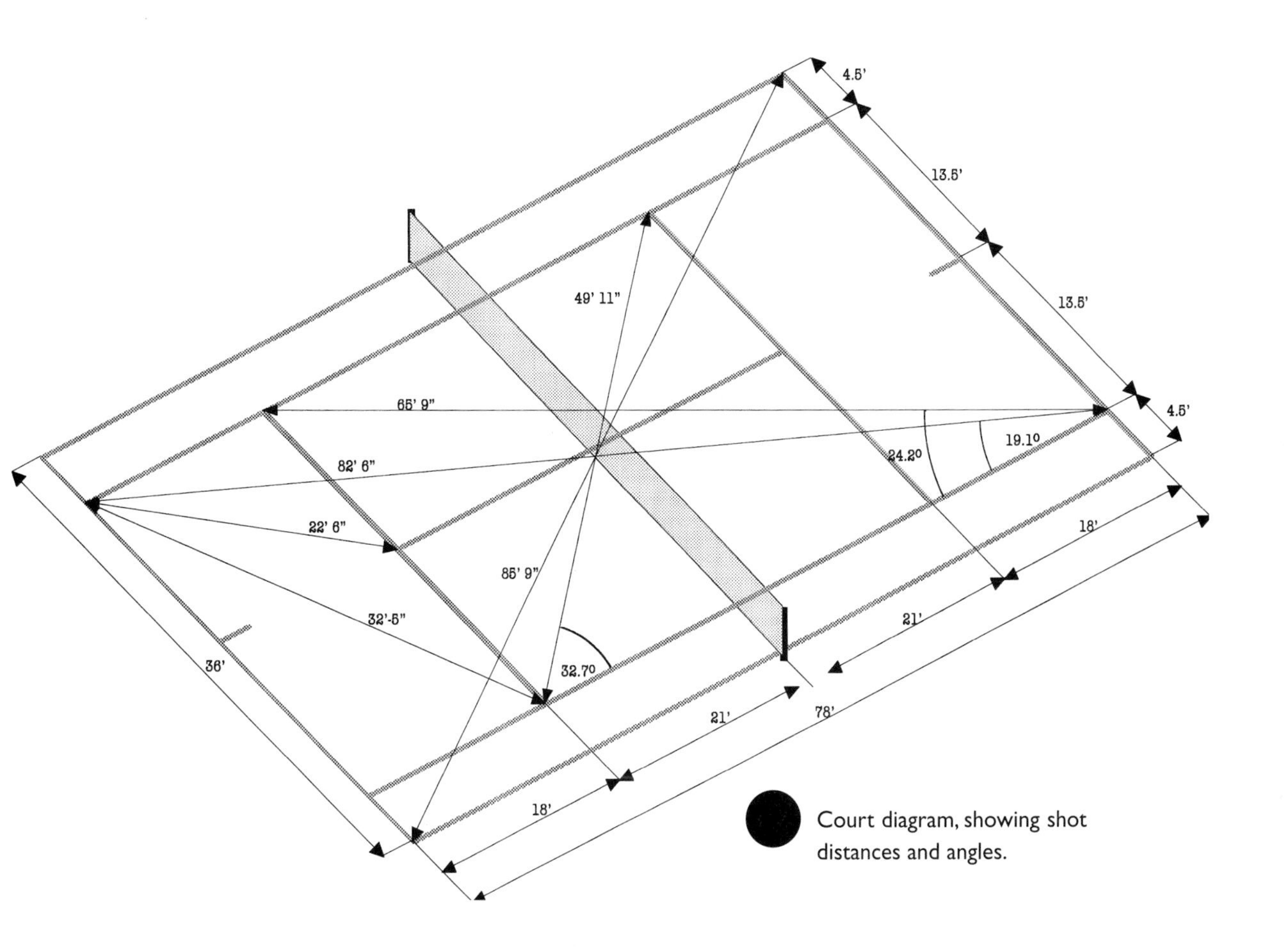

Court diagram, showing shot distances and angles.

Bobby was dying of cancer and I didn't want to bother him, but when Lornie answered the phone, he was next to Bobby's bed with the hospice attendant. Lornie told Bobby my request and he responded, "Tell Vic to go with the story he's printing in his book because I played hundreds of doubles matches alone — and I won." Bobby was under heavy sedation and said he was having trouble recalling the match with Faunce, but that he was sure it happened. "Tell Vic he can use 'on the bench' or 'standing on the side,' whichever is the most colorful." What a character, right down to the end.

This chapter will describe how good doubles players position themselves at the beginning of a point, before the real action begins. This positioning is not to be taken lightly. We'll presume that you're the server, hitting from the right (deuce) side. Also, unless specified, we're talking about right-handed players.

The Server

I have long emphasized the principle that you should serve to the side that statistically will produce the highest and longest return. The higher the return, the easier it is for your team to volley; the longer the ball must travel to stay in play, the less you can be hurt by a short-angle shot.

This means that against most players,

27 Here's a good starting position for all four players at the beginning of a point: the server, the server's partner on his imaginary "X," the receiver, and the partner of the receiver, who stands just behind the service line, halfway between the singles sideline and the center stripe.

most of the time, the goal will be to hit your serve to the opponent's backhand side. So stand where you can hit effectively to the receiver's backhand but close enough to the center stripe that you can cover the empty side of the court when your partner crosses over to poach. Notice that serving down the middle, into the backhand corner, becomes increasingly difficult if you stand more than five feet from the center stripe. The further you move to the right, the less chance there is of getting the ball to your opponent's backhand, even though it hits the backhand corner. (When serving from the left, or ad, court, you can stand a little farther away from the center stripe.)

Later in the book I'll emphasize the fact that with the advent of the two-handed backhand, some people can now return serve on the backhand side lower and harder at your feet than they do off the forehand, so it pays to scout your future opponents and aim accordingly. Also, just serving down the middle, whether it's to a player's forehand or backhand, reduces the return angles and sets up a poach by your partner.

28 At the pro level (here, the Infiniti Open in Los Angeles in 1995), notice how the players are positioned for the start of a typical point. *(Photo: Lisa Marie Roberto)*

29 The server stands comfortably to the left of the center stripe so that he can easily aim for his opponent's backhand side. Notice how the partner of the server is bending forward, ready to break in any direction for the return.

The Partner of the Server

When your partner is serving, you should stand dead center in the service box — at the "X," where the diagonals cross (as seen in photo 30) — ready to move in any direction for the service return, but especially toward the net.

True, sometimes in top tournament competition, the server's partner will stand slightly closer to the center stripe, but if you're at the "X," you're positioned properly for most doubles play. In some cases you can sneak toward the middle, especially from the right side, if your partner can place the serve.

While you might be tempted to station yourself close to the doubles alley to guard against down-the-line returns, this simply allows the other team to hit more easily — and effectively — down the middle of the court. Standing in the center of the service box actually gives your opponent only a narrow opening down the line.

Of course, another reason you may want to plant yourself near the alley, well away from the center stripe, is that you don't trust your partner's serve. This fear leads to

30 The partner of the server should try to be up on his toes as the serve is hit, so that he's ready to break quickly in any direction against the returner's shot.

gigantic arguments, where the net person turns and says, "You dummy, you hit me in the head!" and the server replies, "You toad, you wrecked my best serve!" If you're afraid of getting whacked like this, just bend over so that your head won't be a target. Then if you get hit in the butt, at least your partner knows his serve was going to be a fault anyway.

One new wrinkle I've been seeing in women's pro tennis in recent years is the tandem formation, as demonstrated in photos 31 A–C. Basically, the partner of the server straddles the center stripe and literally squats down, safely below the server's aim and ahead of the service line. As soon as the ball is hit, she rises up and breaks either left or right — obviously trying to confuse her opponents and create hesitation. The serving team has a plan to go one way or the other, but unless it has rehearsed these movements, it often is as confused as the opponents once the ball is in play.

If your team tries to use a tandem formation, the partner of the server must be careful not to get hit by the serve. And the server must learn to cover the empty

A

B

C

31 A–C Against a left-handed receiver, the serving team decides to play tandem formation by having the partner of the server straddle the center line and bend low (A and B). He waits until the serve has passed before breaking in a predetermined direction, as the server comes in and then breaks to his left to cover the open half of the court (C). The server will not normally stand so far to the right because it leaves him such a long distance to go to cover a shot to his left.

32 When the point begins, the partner of the receiver should be standing just behind or just in front of the service line, up on his toes and ready to move forward if his partner hits a strong return. Otherwise, he should either try to hold his ground or retreat.

side of the court as quickly as possible. But what's nice about this change-of-pace alignment is the fact that the opposing team does not know your intentions; you make them uncertain about where to aim their return, which should curb their willingness to poach.

The Service Receiver

Ideally, when you're receiving serve, you should assume a ready position halfway between where the server can run you from forehand to backhand. If she can't break her serve wide to your forehand (serving into the right court), you can "cheat" and stand closer to the center stripe, cutting down her ability to serve to your backhand.

You may wonder, "How do I know how far the range is?" Ideally, you've had a chance to scout your opponents and study how well they serve. Now use the opening games to sense each opponent's serving range and then simply bisect the angle halfway.

The Partner of the Receiver

If you have especially quick reactions and a

33 In a pro tournament, notice how the partner of the server is on his imaginary "X," while the partner of the receiver is just in front of the service line, ready to hold his ground or to attack. *(Photo: Lisa Marie Roberto)*

short backswing on your volley, stand slightly in front of the service line, so that you can better capitalize as a volleyer or respond to a poach by the net person. Should you have slower reactions and a longer volley stroke, stand behind the line. What counts most, however, is your ability to move up quickly and attack when your partner hits a strong service return at the server's feet.

If you're undecided about positioning, avoid standing *on* the line because someday you're going to be so good you'll be playing with line judges, and you may block their view on the serve. Since they can't see through legs, they will ask you to move, forcing you to break under tournament pressure an ingrained habit.

CHAPTER 5

Playing the Four Positions

ONE of the joys of doubles is the ongoing challenge of playing four distinct positions as each set progresses. One moment you're called upon to serve and, ideally, move in to the net; the next moment you're expectantly poised up near the net, hoping that your partner can return serve at the feet of the onrushing server — safely away from the net person, who would just love to tattoo your body with the Wilson logo.

This chapter will explore the responsibilities you have at each position, mostly as an individual, but also within the framework of a team.

The Server

In their seminal book, *The Game of Doubles in Tennis,* first published back in 1956, Bill Talbert and Bruce Old felt it was important to think of the serve in the context of the fact that "in championship doubles play most sets are won by but a single breakthrough of service. . . . In fact, holding service is so vital in doubles that George Lott [argues] that the serve is the most important shot." And since doubles is won by taking and maintaining control of the net, "the successful serve in doubles not only puts the ball in play but also provides a safe journey to the net for the server, putting the serving team in the attacking position at the start of each point."

Interesting, isn't it, how the truisms of this game hold forth decade after decade? Today, when serving in doubles, the most important challenge is still to get the first serve in play as often as possible, even if this means easing off just a bit to help ensure better accuracy. Your team will win a much higher percentage of points when you can consistently get that first serve in, as deep in the service box as possible, so that you can charge the net and not have to rely on a more defensive second serve.

Along with depth, concentrate on serving to the side that produces the highest and longest return from your opponent. A high return, as I pointed out in the previous chapter, makes it easier for you or your partner to hit a putaway volley or an overhead as the two of you rush the net. A long return means that the receiver can't hit short angles at your feet or stretch you wide as you're moving forward from the baseline. This results in a return that's much easier to handle and gives your team an opportunity to end the point early.

In singles, especially at the club level, an opponent's weaker side on the service return has traditionally been the backhand, but this doesn't hold true as often in today's doubles. For one thing, many players have acquired two-handed backhands over the past 15 or 20 years, making them more dangerous here than from the forehand side. Meanwhile, the player who hits the ball "flat," with a one-handed, across-the-body swing, produces a shot that is normally weak in singles but potentially effective in doubles, because it travels low and barely clears the net, thus producing a more difficult shot to volley.

Today, if you consciously aim your serve to the backhand, do so because the player is usually late on the ball and thus has a tendency to underspin the return and raise the ball. A ball hit with underspin is going to travel longer on a straighter line, and not dip over the net as it does with topspin, making it easier for your team to advance to the net and volley. In order to hit a topspin backhand — the return everyone fears — the receiver must contact the ball farther out in front of the body than on the forehand. Most people tend to be late doing this and, as a result, must resign themselves to hitting the ball flat or with underspin, minimizing their offensive potential.

Another reason for concentrating on serving to the receiver's backhand when he's in the deuce (right) court is that he must swing out away from the body in order to hit a ball that eludes the opposing net player. Hitting away from the body like this is difficult, going opposite the natural, across-the-body tendency, and usually forces the receiver to hit with underspin. (Backhands are less of a problem from the ad court, since the tendency to pull across the body produces a shot that travels away from your partner at the net.)

There are two times when you should aim away from your opponent's weaker side: (1) when he is "overplaying" that side so much that you are positive you can ace him with a serve he can't reach, even on his stronger side, and (2) when you are positive you can pull him so far out of court that you produce a weak return.

If your opponent doesn't seem to have a weaker side, try to serve consistently down the middle and deep. This minimizes his potential to hurt you with short-angle, crosscourt returns from either side, since he must lengthen those angles in order to hit the ball hard and keep it in play.

Attack the Net!

Be aggressive in your thinking as you prepare to serve. Remember, this is your opportunity to start a point with your team in control of the net, where the majority of points will be won or lost. So you should try to advance behind your serve — even a

A

B

C

D

E

34 A–E On a practice court, the server is working on his check, or split, step. In photo A, he completes step number one (landing on the left foot). In photo B, he lengthens his second step's stride. Then he begins to bring his feet together in a split-step motion (C). It's extremely important that he avoid making a complete stop with his split step, but, rather, do only a balancing act, a slowing down. His center of gravity should still be moving forward as he lands (D) and then moves into the net for a potential volley (E).

weak first serve — and join your partner at the net. If you stay back and leave him stranded up there, smart opponents are going to move in behind their return and give him a "new look" by the end of the match.

Of course, if you're a slow runner and your serve is even slower, stay at the baseline and encourage your partner to fall back and join you. Then pray that the point lasts long enough for the two of you to lob and drive your opponents away from the net.

After contacting the ball and as you fall into the court, keep moving forward, as photos 34 A–E show. On the third step, momentarily bring your feet together square to the net, ready to break in any direction to handle the service return. *But keep moving!* Taking this check step, or split step, just before the receiver strikes the ball — without actually coming to a complete stop — will keep you balanced and enable you to move with equal ease to your right or left, depending on where the return goes.

Coming to a complete halt on the check step raises a serious problem as you prepare to cover the return. What you must determine in practice is how fast you can still be moving forward when you take the check step and still move laterally with ease. (If you're slow coming in behind your serve, you may actually have to bring your feet together on the second step in order to be ready to break when the ball is hit.) In some cases, players have to actually stop, but most players realize that this isn't necessary and that it keeps them from getting deep for the volley. Players who completely stop normally relax their muscles and must recruit them again to move laterally — a slow process that normally results in having to hit lower volleys from a position further from the net than desired.

What are the barriers, psychological and physical, that might be keeping you from attacking the net behind your serve?

Perhaps you have a perception that reflects the challenge I received from a woman when I gave a clinic in Snowmass, Colorado. She said, "Vic, when I serve and go in, my opponents nail the ball at my feet and I lose a lot of points. I think I'm better off just staying back."

I learned that the woman actually had a strong serve and could move well, so I said, "Wait a minute — you missed one critical part of the system. When you serve, how often does your partner poach and try to bother your opponents on the service return?"

"Well, never," she replied, meaning that her partner was ignoring a critical tactical weapon by failing to break early across the court for an anticipated volley at the net.

"So," I said, in a friendly manner, "don't abandon my strategy until you've tried a tactic like poaching. You can't let the receiver stand back there and pound away at your serve, knowing that you're never coming to the net or that your partner is never going to move early and poach. Your partner has to force the receiver to think about hitting a different shot, in a different direction, by poaching several times, even if her volleys are unsuccessful. Even fake poaches can be effective at distracting the receiver as she goes to hit the return."

I continued, "You'll often be stunned at how quickly a player can come unraveled when confronted with new and unexpected pressure against a comfortable shot

35 The server (foreground) is moving across to cover the vacated side of the court as his partner breaks to poach the opponent's service return.

she normally hits with confidence. Be quite surprised if she easily adjusts. When people have a format and never have to make a change when they hit, then you help make them great. But when you disrupt that format, amazing things can happen. Of course, if you try these things and still keep losing too many points, then stay back and try to win from the baseline."

A lack of good volleying technique could also be inhibiting you from rushing the net behind your serve, because you're scared you will miss the low return at your feet as it comes up off the court. You may be fine on volleys you can contact from waist to head level, but when the ball is down around your ankles, forcing you to bend low, you're in deep trouble.

Here's where it pays to learn to volley from the shoulder instead of the forearm, hitting straight into the incoming flight pattern of the ball with a slight lift if necessary, instead of opting for a chopping underspin type of stroke. Always remember, the variables that need to be calculated and controlled when you try to hit with underspin are many times greater than when you contact the ball with a flat stroking motion, the racket traveling on the same flight pattern from which the ball arrives.

While technique problems are certainly

A

B

36 A–B Moving in from the baseline to hit a half-volley, this player gets low and keeps the racket tilted slightly forward (or downward) as he hits with shoulder action, as opposed to "scooping" the ball with a wrist motion (A). He rises up as he hits and keeps moving forward with his racket high so that he's ready for a follow-up volley closer to the net (B).

an inhibiting factor here, it helps to remember that not every service return is going to challenge you as a low, hard volley or half-volley. We tend to recall Bertha's "return of a lifetime" shot, not the 10 "floaters" she sends back to a server who's moving in and can volley.

In addition, ask yourself this: "Just how effectively am I actually moving toward the net after I serve? Am I getting deep enough to contact my opponent's return waist high or above, as often as possible?" A good server's goal is to get inside the service line for his or her first volley. This will guarantee a higher volleying position. I once saw Sweden's Stefan Edberg go over the net with his follow-through on his first volley. It's true that the service return was mis-hit and slow, but in any case, that's moving.

You may think you're simply too slow to play this way, but quickness and speed afoot may not actually be the culprits. The problem could be traced to your serving technique if you're contacting the ball up above your head, instead of out in front of your body, off the hitting side (as is contrasted in photos 37 A–B and 38). Tossing the ball forward allows your body to be moving toward the net as you make contact. But a ball toss that goes straight up keeps your center of gravity over the baseline at impact, delaying your move to the net. Notice in the photographs how much further the server advances after hitting the ball out in front than the player who makes contact straight over his head. The first player will normally be able to volley the ball at chest level, while player 2 will be forced to volley off her feet, against the same shot from a ball machine. That's a critically different challenge.

Nor should a relatively slow serve necessarily inhibit you from moving

37 A–B This woman is practicing having her service toss travel out in front of her body, off her hitting shoulder (A), so that she's already on the way to the net as she follows through (B). Her goal is to reach the final box on her third step (the check step), at which point her opponent should be returning the ball so she can break in the appropriate direction.

A

B

38 In this service drill, by keeping her service toss out in front of her body, the server in the foreground is able to fall into the court on her follow-through, as contrasted to player 2, who has tossed the ball straight up and must complete the serve before moving forward.

39 As the serve passes to his left, the partner of the server prestretches his leg muscles by rising up on his toes so that he's ready to move quickly to a ball within his range.

40 The partner of the server rises up on his toes in anticipation of the service return coming his way.

forward, provided you contact the ball out in front and advance with good footwork. After all, the ball is taking longer to reach the receiver, which allows you more time to move in to the net. In fact, when Pancho Gonzales began playing Ken Rosewall on their tour many years ago, he found he wasn't getting in far enough against Rosewall's lethal returns, so he adjusted by simply serving at three-quarter speed. This allowed him more time to move in deeper and volley more effectively, while still keeping pressure on Rosewall with his great serve.

A

The Server's Partner

Playing the net when your partner is serving can prove to be a lot of fun or a ball-pocked disaster for your body, depending upon your volleying skills and your partner's ability — and willingness — to come in behind his serve and support you.

Remember, at the start of the point you should be standing in the center of the service court, concentrating, ready to make your move. Once you're in a good ready position — crouched down low so that your head doesn't ruin your partner's best serve — look ahead at your opponent and try to sense what type of shot he will try to hit. Looking back to see what your partner is doing is not only unnecessary but dangerous. Instead, the moment you hear the racket hit the ball, rise up on the balls of your feet, set your racket, and prepare to move in either direction to pick off the return of serve. Too often, players freeze in their crouch and aren't prepared to hit the ball when it comes to them.

Now study the receiver's racket in order to anticipate a drive or a lob.

If the moving racket is on the same level

B

41 A–B Up at the net, learn to "read" your opponent's body movements and racket action for clues that he's either going to drive the ball (A) or attempt to lob it over your head (B). A player's left hand usually gives away the lob.

as the intended point of impact with the ball, look for a drive, since nobody is talented enough to suddenly lower the racket and lob. This means you should have the confidence and aggressiveness to break forward on the diagonal to cut off the shot near the net. Against a fairly high ball, try to angle your volley quickly off the court for a winner. When the return has been hit well and forces you to volley from a fairly deep position, think more about going deep and down the middle.

If you see your opponent's racket head drop below the oncoming ball with a beveled face, it's going to be a lob, and you should turn and take three quick steps back before even looking up for the ball.

When studying your opponent's racket, try to have just one thought in mind: "The next ball that's hit is mine; wherever it goes, I'm going to try to get it." You should be thinking that you own the fortress — from net post to net post — against any drive the receiver hits, and you shouldn't feel guilty about having this attitude or worry about being called a ball hog. Remember, you're in a better position than your partner to hit a winning volley; you're closer to the net and you can hit a sharper angle. But to earn and justify that advantage, you must be determined to get that fast first step toward the ball.

Timid volleyers rarely think about getting a jump like this. When the point begins, they tend to settle into their ready position near the net and refuse to move until it's too late to be effective. They're so fearful of misreading their opponent's shot or reluctant to commit to taking their own shot that they freeze in that classic ready pose: heels flat, butt out, and the racket up in front of their face. They're not about to move until absolutely forced to do so.

Instead of camping in a ready position like this, stay up on your toes, prepared to break in any direction to field the service return. After all, this is only a momentary starting position from which it is unlikely you will ever hit a ball.

Now, what to do if you have a partner who serves and never joins you at the net? Here's my tennis and medical advice: Either move back to the baseline or dump your partner. Otherwise, halfway through the first set against a good team you're going to have ball bruises all over your body from trying to play up at the net alone. If you retreat to join your partner at the baseline as he prepares to serve, he very likely will ask you rather indignantly, "What are you doing here?" Simply tell him, "I want to live."

How to Thrive as a Poacher

Poaching is an art, occurring when the player at the net crosses over early to the server's side to volley the anticipated or predictable return. This is an increasingly popular tactic that can distract and unnerve the person receiving serve, while giving your team the potential to strike swiftly for a winner. Of course, it also requires good timing and communication, so that your poaching intentions are clear and your partner can cover your vacated side of the court. Without teamwork — and camouflage — you'll get burned by an alert team that hits down the alley behind you for a winner every time you poach.

To avoid getting burned like this, you should signal your partner — the server — that you're going to poach. Either talk to each other before each point or simply give a little signal behind your back — just like the pros do, even at Wimbledon. For example, one finger behind the back means

42 The partner of the server poaches successfully here, breaking across early to cut off player 2's crosscourt backhand return. Note how the server has switched and is moving across to cover his partner's side of the court. Always remember in this situation: Once the poacher's foot crosses the center line, he's responsible for that side of the court.

43 This net player is signaling her intention to poach or to fake a poach on the next serve.

you're going to poach if the first serve lands in — but only on the first serve. Two fingers means "I'm poaching only on the second serve." An open hand indicates "I'm going on any serve that lands in." And a clenched fist warns "I'm not going anywhere, but I might fake it."

Just make sure you keep your intentions hidden from your opponents. Too often I see people at the net turn around, with their signal still in place behind their back, and ask, "Did you get that, George?" Also, be aware that while you are busy signaling, your partner may be so wrapped up in his own serve that he doesn't even notice your signals.

The longer you and your partner play together, the more able you should be to rely on each other's poaching instincts. On nearly all the great teams, neither player has to signal because they have played together so long that each person knows: If the serve is hit to a particular location, the poacher automatically has the right to break all the way across the court. They've discussed this, and the server knows that if he serves to a certain location, his partner is automatically going to poach.

If you intend to poach, you cannot move too soon or you'll give away the plot. Just wait until the receiver starts his swing forward into the ball, then go, because a player can't effectively change his swing on the return once he's committed to a crosscourt shot. Meanwhile, you still make the return more difficult to execute by providing a distraction at the net that may cause the receiver to hurry the shot or lift his head too early and make an error. (If you're new to the game and eager to poach, make sure you know the rules. One day I watched the partner of the receiver poach against the serve, but she volleyed the ball before it even bounced to her partner, which, of course, though an intriguing tactic, is totally illegal.)

When your partner knows that you are going to poach, his challenge is to cover your side of the court as you move to cut off the return. After he serves, he shouldn't immediately run to cover the vacated alley behind you since this will give away the poach. Instead, he should advance toward the net like he normally would, taking two steps forward after his follow-through before breaking crosscourt when he sees the receiver committing himself to a return. He can then cover any down-the-line shot.

If you poach correctly but still occasionally get burned down the alley, don't abandon the tactic. Just make sure that you are not tipping off your intentions too early. Rare are the potential opponents who can consistently aim the ball behind you and keep it in play. Much more often, good poaching will give your team an important edge — even if your partner has a relatively weak serve.

The Service Receiver

The return of serve in doubles could well be the most demanding shot to hit effectively in tennis — particularly if you're a right-hander hitting a backhand from the deuce court with a tall opponent at the net. Not only must you know how to execute a backhand return, you must keep it away from the net person, which gre[illegible] your target-area opportunities ([illegible] to in singles, where you can utilize the opponent's entire court for your return).

While getting the ball back and keeping

44 A–D The server's job is to get right to the net as fast as possible. But wait! The server sees his brilliant partner beginning to poach (B), and now he must cover his partner's side. If his partner gave signals that he will poach, it's critical that the server not telegraph the play by immediately crossing to his partner's side, because this gives the opposition a quick clue to hit down the line on the service return. In photo C, the poacher is [illegible] and moving fast because he now has complete responsibility for the other side. In photo D, the server [illegible]de it, and his partner is ready for the ball way ahead of time; he could set up a tent on this one.

45 The service returner moves aggressively forward and nails the ball crosscourt at the server's feet.

the point alive is certainly crucial, ultimately you should be returning serve with a specific purpose. Try to have an ideal target area in mind — the outside corner of the crosscourt service box (as photo 45 shows). If you can drive your return close to that area with a reasonable amount of pace and fairly close to the net tape, you will accomplish two things: (1) you'll avoid giving the net player an easy high ball to poach, and (2) you'll give the server — if he's coming to the net — a difficult shot to volley.

Of course, if you can actually hit this kind of shot consistently, send me a postcard from Wimbledon, but at least you're focusing on a specific goal.

When you prepare to receive serve, in doubles just as in singles, move back far enough that you can immediately step forward as the serve heads your way, instead of getting forced back by the serve's unexpected speed. Strange as it may sound, you can move two steps forward as quickly as you can take one step backward, so you're actually saving time by playing deep enough to move directly to the ball. Plus, you're already advancing to the net if you hit a successful return.

Since you're striving to keep ll away from the net player, the s urn of serve in doubles is normally t crosscourt drive, which also gives most court in which to land the b

46 When receiving serve, instead of settling in on your heels as the ball approaches, prestretch your calf muscles by rising up on the balls of your feet. This facilitates a fast first step into the ball.

There's often a temptation to go down the line, past the net player, but unless you see him moving to poach, your best percentage return is to hit it crosscourt, away from his reach.

Go[illegible]ber two should be either to hit the ba[illegible] feet of the onrushing server — w[illegible]ch forces him to hit up — or drive hi[illegible] into the alley, in order to open [illegible]rt for a subsequent volley by you or your partner. Crunching the return hard and deep can feel good, but this usually gives the server an easy volley if he follows his serve to the net, as most good doubles players try to do.

When you can land your return around the server's feet, be ready to scurry forward and join your partner at the net. The server will have to play the ball defensively from below the tape of the net; so look for a

A

B

47 A–B The classic challenge for every service returner is to lay the ball back at the feet of ... (A) and then follow the path of that shot to the net (B), ready to volley the server's shot from ... tape.

high, floating shot that you can attack with an aggressive revolley.

If you have a particularly weak backhand and can only rarely hit the ball at the server's feet or drive him wide, don't give the point away by simply hitting the ball toward the net person with hopes that he will somehow muff the shot. At least make your opponents earn the point. One approach is to run around a troublesome backhand and hit your forehand as often as possible. Also, prepare earlier, so that you have time simply to block the ball back toward the server, allowing his shot to provide the power. And don't forget the lob, which can drive your opponents back as your team takes over the net.

Taking the Ball on the Rise

One of my research studies emphasizes how important it can be to take the ball on the rise when receiving serve in doubles, as opposed to staying way back and hitting the ball on its downflight. You don't necessarily hit the ball harder by taking the ball early. What you gain is a reduction in your opponent's reaction time and his ability to reach the ball and hit a good shot when he's coming in behind his serve.

There's a choice here. If your opponent (the server) lacks foot speed and quickness, you should move quickly to the ball, take it on the rise and try to force him to come in for his shot. If mobility isn't his problem, then you should buy time for your return by moving back to take the serve on the downflight, after it bounces. However, still make [illegible]u're moving forward into the shot [illegible]t.

U[illegible]izing [illegible] Short-Angle Return

A critical shot in good doubles is the soft, short-angle service return — hit flat, with topspin, or with underspin and either wide to the alley or just over the net at the net-rushing server. A shot like this stays low once it hits the court and is tough to handle. Even if the server can reach the ball, he can't hit an attacking shot because the ball is too low, beneath the level of the top of the net. Hitting a lob from here is equally difficult and risks giving your team an overhead opportunity.

This means that if you can execute dink returns, you and your partner should capitalize by aggressively charging the net together, ready to volley a weak return (while remaining on the move as you hit) or step up and slam an overhead.

While dink returns can indeed give the opposing team fits, they obviously need to be mixed in with drives to keep your opponents guessing. Otherwise the opposing net player will feel free to cut across early to volley, correctly anticipating the dink and obviously nullifying the shot's advantages. The server will also capitalize by simply slowing up as he rushes the net and allowing the ball to bounce up, then killing it, instead of having to move in deep for a little low ball at his feet.

Moreover, most pros today, when they have enough time against the serve (especially on the forehand side), try to hit hard topspin returns so that the ball arcs down as it crosses the net. Boris Becker, for one, can take a hard-hit serve and still nail a topspin return, giving him a lethal weapon. When you hit like this with topspin, you can drive the ball hard and still keep it in play, as opposed to hitting flat or with underspin, which requires you to take speed off the ball, because it won't dip but will stay higher over the net. Also, a topspin return is still low to the court against the net rusher and forces him into a low

48 This player is concentrating on the ball and keeping her head still as she returns the serve down the line, foiling a poaching attempt by her opponent at the net as the server rushes over to cover the poacher's side of the court. When trying to hit behind the poacher, keep your head down as you swing and don't be distracted by his movement; otherwise you'll tend to pull the ball in his direction.

49 Just to keep the net person honest, the service returner will occasionally drive the ball at the net person, hoping either to catch the person poaching or cause a weak volley return.

volley that is difficult to control because the ball is dipping.

How to Outfox the Poacher

Avoid predictability not only by mixing up your drives and dinks when returning serve but by hitting shots designed to foil a poacher. If the opposing net player learns to sense where you are going to try to hit the ball every time, he'll be emboldened to poach and will pick off all but your best crosscourt returns.

The best way to foil a poacher when you anticipate the poach or see him leave his position too early and move crosscourt — before you've started your intended swing — is to hit a down-the-alley return behind him, toward his vacated position (as in photo 48). He won't be able to stop and recover to reach your shot, and the server will have to run a long way to cover for him. A second choice is the lob, since both opponents are moving (the net person poaching and the server covering the poacher's vacated side of the court) and could be caught in awkward positions. Or, drive the ball down the middle as they are shifting.

Whatever you decide, don't panic. Pick your shot, aim, and hit, since second-guessing will simply play into the poacher's hand. If you're keeping an eye on the opposing netman and thinking, "I'll hit it to his forehand side. . . . No, there he goes, I'll hit it behind him," the confusion can easily cause you to mis-hit the return. UCLA's motor-learning expert Dick Schmidt told me that an individual needs about one-fifth of a second to override a command to the brain (i.e., change your mind), and thus, if a tennis shot is already approaching, there's simply not enough

A

B

50 A–B V[illegible]en your opponent poaches to the cente[illegible] [illegible]r your predictable crosscourt return (A)[illegible] [illegible]rn to lob so that you can foil him by g[illegible] [illegible]eep in either corner (B).

time for the brain to reprogram the muscles successfully.

If the opposing net player doesn't give away his intentions to poach by leaving too early, try occasionally to hit a hard shot at his right hip (because it's virtually impossible for a player to get a racket on this type of shot and hit a lucky winner) — or down the alley to keep him honest, even if he doesn't poach. This will let him know that you have this capability and you're not afraid to use it, even if you guess wrong and he wins the point. That may convince him to stay at home more often or make him hesitate before poaching the next time around.

Another "keep 'em guessing" shot (especially from the left, or ad, court) is the lob, aimed deep to the server's backhand corner. This is particularly valuable when you have trouble hitting a forceful, down-the-line backhand behind the poaching net player, who's anticipating your normal crosscourt shot. A good lob takes him out of the action and forces a long retrieving effort by the server if he's already on his way to the net.

One common problem to avoid here is worrying about what your opponent at the net is doing as you go to hit. When you think too much ("I'll trick him with this shot by hitting behind him"), that's when your partner usually has to walk to the net to retrieve your ball. I'll admit, it's human nature to look out of the corner of your eye as you're swinging the racket, wondering what that bum is doing on the other side of the net. Yet, the answer is, he can't do anything until you hit, because there's only one ball in play — and you own it. So keep your head down through impact and your eyes on the ball. Turning the head too early disturbs the swing and can cause the racket to travel on a horizontal plane, which in turn helps send the ball into the net.

If your service returns continually catch the net or fall woefully short when you want to go deep, remember that gravity is affecting the ball much more than you might think. In scientific studies with University of Pennsylvania physicist Howard Brody, we compared two shots hit against a 100-m.p.h. serve that is traveling just 50 m.p.h. when it reaches the baseline.

One ball left the service return hitter's vertical racket face at a 10-degree upward angle (struck from a 3-foot height), cleared the net by 1.5 feet, and landed at the service line on the opponent's side — a perfect return if the server is attacking. Against the same serve, a ball hit at 15 degrees up from horizontal cleared the net by 4.8 feet and landed 5 feet inside the opponent's baseline — perfect if the server is staying back. In both cases the racket was traveling 25 m.p.h. at impact. This experiment also emphasizes how important it is to hit with a low-to-high stroking motion that lifts the ball to counteract the effects of gravity. This allows you to hit the ball hard but keep it in play.

Defending Against the Tandem Formation

If your opponents serve from the tandem formation (both of them on or near the center line), the best tip-off of their intention to break left or right is usually the server. He knows he must cover the side left unprotected by his partner and usually moves over on the second step after serving because he's so doggone worried about how far he has to move laterally. A nervous, less experienced player will often reveal this intention on the first step, which will give you time to make a decision with your return as you see the ball coming.

Of course, against a big-time server who may be cranking the ball at 100 m.p.h., you only have time to think instantly and aim one way or the other with your return. An opponent at the net, playing in the tandem formation, is going to break one way or the other, but the faster you can return the serve, the less time that person will have to make a decision and the fewer steps he can take toward the ball. So a good return is important.

The Partner of the Receiver

I talked earlier (page 47) about that common tennis phenomenon at the club level, where both teams are playing "one up, one back" doubles. In this scenario, the partner of the receiver feels he has nothing to do except watch his partner rally with the server until one of them makes an error. Yet very often, of course, a shot suddenly comes to this spectator player, who invariably dumps it into the net because he wasn't prepared.

Instead of resigning yourself to a passive role as the receiver's partner, camping on one side of the court and watching all the action, you should focus on the fact that in good doubles you can make your team famous. If your partner can return the serve safely away from the netman, everything may now depend on how well you can "read" the server's intentions and move to cover his subsequent shot. When you can anticipate this shot and get a quick jump, you're in the best position on the court to put the ball away for a winner.

Here again, though, you must be primed

to trust your instincts, get a fast first step, and not remain immobilized once the point begins, simply because you're too enamored with your ready position and you can't make up your mind.

You very likely have played with a person like this. He hunkers down at the net and is quite comfortable as he watches the action. When a ball comes near him, he's thinking, "Is it to my backhand or my forehand? . . . It was to my forehand," as he watches the ball go by without budging an inch. Then another ball comes and goes right by him, and he says, "Nuts! I should have gone." So now he really gets stoked up and is telling himself, "If I don't run the next time, I will be an idiot." Then the ball comes and he says, "Yours!" He's still in his ready position and he hasn't even lifted his heels.

Don't let yourself fall into that trap; be ready to get involved from the very beginning of the point. When your opponent serves, you should be standing about halfway up the court, just in front of or behind the service line, ready to call the serve "out" if it is long or wide. (Most players stand behind the line, especially today, as the ball moves faster with the new rackets. They feel they can have a better chance to return the shot of the poaching partner of the server. Some pros prefer to stand inside the line, but they are the ones with extremely fast hands and feet. Also, the partners of the best service returners have confidence to move inside the line, because they seldom get hit by the poaching partner of the server.)

If the serve lands in, quickly turn and look at the net person — the potential poacher — so that you're ready to play his shot if he goes. If he stays put, look for the

A

B

51 A–B The partner of the receiver is in the best position to call the service line for his partner (A), but then he can waste no time in repositioning his eyes to his opponents as he prepares to play his position (B).

52 Whenever an opponent is hitting a ball from below net level, you and your partner should attack.

server, and if he's charging in with a big smile on his face and waving his racket over his head as he prepares to deck the ball, you know your partner has hit a lousy return and it's time to retreat for your life.

However, if your partner has done his job by returning the ball away from the net person and near the feet of the onrushing server, that player must bend down and play the ball defensively with a low or half-volley to get it over the net. Rarely will he be able to hit it hard — and keep it in play — or lob it successfully over your head. So now is the time to earn your keep by rushing in confidently from your midcourt position to attack anything within reach. As the member of your team who is closer to the net, you have priority — and the better opportunity — to move in and put away the volley. In fact, you should be thinking that any ball the server hits back is yours, from net post to net post, and this means moving without hesitation to end the point right now.

One skill you'll need to develop here is an ability to read the racket face of the server who is bending low to hit a half-volley or volley. If the racket head is parallel to the net, jump forward to volley; if it is angled crosscourt, break for your partner's territory. Learn to react instinctively, so that you avoid staying glued to your "X" as you try to make a decision. This is something you can practice by having a person hit half-volleys as you analyze whether he's going down the line or crosscourt while you also try to cut off his shot. Also, some players are quite good at gathering and using statistical data; for example, what shot the server hits coming in on what point.

Strategically, when things aren't going well for your team on the service return, you may want to give your opponents a different look by staying back with your partner on the serve. But this is a last-resort tactic that seldom works, for you're admitting to your opponents that you have elected to play defensively from the baseline and that your only hope is for them to miss shots. In Davis Cup competition against Sweden in 1994, U.S. captain Tom Gullikson suggested at one point that his doubles players, Jared Palmer and Jonathan Stark, stay back on the return to take pressure off the returner and then try to get the ball in play rather than attempt a spectacular return. Alas, "It didn't help much," wrote Julie Cart of the *Los Angeles Times,* as Palmer and Stark lost in four sets.

CHAPTER 6

Teamwork and Strategy

WHILE every player has individual challenges and responsibilities in doubles, certainly the beauty of this game — and the key to beating players of comparable ability — is teamwork, for a fluid pair beats the team that is hesitant and confused almost every time. Let's explore the many team principles that should shape your strategy and will determine your success as you try to beat those bums across the net.

Move Together as a Team

Unless the ball is coming back down the center, drawing you and your partner together to cover the shot, try to move in tandem, about 10 to 12 feet apart, as though connected by a rope. If your partner rushes the net, be ready to follow him in; if he goes left, head left; if he goes right, break right; if you see a lob coming, both of you should turn and retreat immediately. The court can be covered quite effectively when the two of you are always in sync like this.

While the court is 36 feet wide in doubles (as compared to 27 feet in singles), each player has to cover only 18 feet laterally — if he or she moves in tandem with his or her partner. Moreover, it's hard to pass two players, either down the line or between them, when they know how to shift with the ball.

If you hit to the right side or to the left, overload that side to cut off the angle of your opponent's return. When one of you hits down the center, both of you should be ready to cover the center. You may feel you're leaving yourself unprotected on the flanks, but if you ever play a team that can

53 A doubles team should always strive to stay about 10 to 12 feet apart as it moves to cover a shot.

54 The targets are tight and dangerous when hitting from the baseline against a team that closes off the middle.

55 These teammates hold a rope between them as they practice what it means to cover the court in tandem about 10 1/2 feet apart.

consistently hit the ball into that narrow target area — the doubles alleys — I'll show you two players who are on their way to Wimbledon.

Learning to shift together as a team takes practice and communication, but I would avoid the drill I tried — once — many years ago. I talked two of my students into tying themselves together with a rope, 10 1/2 feet apart, so they could sense what it meant to maintain that distance between themselves as they tried to keep the rope taut in a "shadow tennis" type of drill. I had to drop the idea, though, after they practically yanked each other apart when one player said "Drive!" and the other cried "Lob!" and they broke in opposite directions.

When actually playing a match, what should you do if your team is suddenly caught "one up, one back" during a rally, when your partner mistakenly retreats to the baseline while you're at the net? Instead of moving back to join your partner, I'd advise you to poach on the very next shot. Invariably, the other team thinks, "We've got them — just keep it deep and attack," but they very often hit the ball too carefully toward your partner's side of the court. This gives you, the poacher, a putaway opportunity as you break crosscourt for a volley. If you fail to play aggressively like this, your opponents will take the net, and you're going to get juiced. (Conversely, if you catch the opposing team in "one up, one back" disarray, hit the next ball deep to the opponent at the baseline, away from the net player, and move in together to take control of the net. Percentage-wise, this is a safer ploy than going for the player at the net, if he already has position; he may hit a lucky winner just by virtue of being close to the net.)

Communicate

Communicating out loud with your partner is the best method I know to help coordinate reactions and movements as a team. Both of you should learn to call out "It's a drive!" or "It's a lob!" while breaking for the ball. At first you may be a little self-conscious, and there will be times when your partner calls out "drive" just as you yell "lob," and the two of you run in different directions. But after you've played together for a while, you should begin to react instinctively, so that when the ball is hit — *boom!* — you're both moving as a team. To develop this teamwork, however, neither of you can be reluctant to call out advice that can help your partner and your team. This verbalizing may require a conscious effort if it goes against your basic personality or you've grown up believing that tennis is a genteel sport and you're not supposed to talk to your partner while the point is being played. But I've found that when a team is communicating out loud — "Switch!" "Cover!" "Back!" — each player feels a greater responsibility to get a quick jump on the ball. When both players are yelling and forcing themselves to call the shot, the player who tends to react later than his partner will start working harder at anticipating a drive or a lob, assuming he has the barest sense of teamwork *and* he wants to hit his legitimate share of shots that come between them.

In recent years I've also noticed that the pros, men and women alike, talk to one another between almost every point; rather than rely on signals, they meet at the "T" and discuss what they're going to do on the next point (e.g., poach) or mull over strategy that may or may not be working. This makes sense. You don't have to talk with your partner between every point, but you need to have a system worked out so that you each know what the other is going to do. This relieves a lot of potential stress, in the sense that there are no surprises on your side of the net. If your team is serving and you've decided to poach, you and your partner are both ready to move decisively, while the other team can only guess your intentions.

Keep in mind the stress studies by scientists in San Francisco who were able to measure chemically the rise and fall of an individual's anxiety levels. They found that people who have advance knowledge of potential events have less stress. Translated into tennis, this means that better performance takes place when there's an absence of uncertainty. So, when you talk as a team, plotting tactics, and you respect each other's role and responsibilities, there are no surprises — no court-hog antics — and it's wonderful, because you play with less stress. The more certain you are of what's going to happen, the less stress there is and the more appropriate your movements are. Conversely, when one partner is a court hog who tries to play beyond her abilities, there is constant indecision. She may know

56 Doubles is a game of constant movement. If your partner is flat-footed as he watches the action unfold, think about finding his successor.

what she's going to do, but her partner has no clue, and this person's anxiety is going to translate into confusion, poor performance, and the realization, "I hate to play with that person."

Stay on the Move

One reason why avid singles players are reluctant to commit to doubles is their perception that doubles fails to offer enough exercise. I'll admit, doubles action is pretty slow and intermittent the way many people play. For instance, when a rookie player reaches a good position near the net, he thinks, "Made it!" He's so happy about gaining the threshold that he's not about to budge until the ball actually comes his way. So instead of staying up on his toes, ready to break in any direction, he settles down on his heels and suddenly becomes quite comfortable, and a hypnosis settles in as he watches the ball go back and forth between the two deep players.

In good doubles, if you're standing still for two shots, you've probably committed a serious error. You and your partner should always be moving in unison — up, back, or laterally — committing yourselves almost automatically the instant you sense a drive or a lob. Even if your partner beats you to a shot you thought was yours, be ready to break hard for the very next ball. This approach to the game will keep your heart pumping at a nice rate, keep you involved, and help your team win more matches.

Concentrate on Hitting down the Middle

When your team is volleying near the net or has been forced backcourt, try to concentrate on hitting down the middle between your opponents. Occasionally you'll want to drill the ball directly at a particularly weak volleyer, but unless you have one of your opponents set up for the kill, or an open target area on their court, or an absolute putaway down an alley, aim for the center stripe.

First, this tactic splits the opposing team and can create some confusion, as you bring your opponents together with that familiar scenario: "Yours!" "Mine!" *Crash!*

Second, the net is about four and a half inches lower in the center than it is at the singles sidelines, meaning less risk for hitting errors when you contact the ball near the center stripe.

And third, you will cut down your opponents' effective volleying angles if they get to the ball.

The pros drive the alleys only if they think an opponent is going to poach against a ball down the center or if they want to penalize their opponents for overplaying the middle.

Protect the Middle

Meanwhile, when the ball is on the other side of the net, your concern should always be to protect the middle — even "cheating"

57 When a team is overly concerned about "guarding the alleys," a hitter from the baseline has an easy drive right up the middle.

58 A smart team closes off the middle as it takes control of the net, illustrated by two pros in the 1995 Infiniti Open in Los Angeles. *(Photo: Lisa Marie Roberto)*

in that direction through positioning and anticipation — since a strong team is going to hit down the center at every opportunity. In fact, if you hear your opponents whisper, "Watch your alley," this is a tip-off that they have a significant flaw in their tactical thinking. When they try to compensate for their fear that your team is continually going to hit down the line from the backcourt, one opponent will play wide to the left side and the other wide to the right. But this leaves them one person short. They're so intent on guarding their alleys, you could drive a truck between them.

Well-versed opponents, in contrast, will concentrate on attacking your middle because (1) the net is lower in the center, (2) their shot may create confusion and cause you and your partner to clash rackets or hesitate in going for the ball, and (3) they know you won't be able to sharply angle your return volley. So be ready!

When your team is at the net, try to "hug" the center of the court a little bit, tempting your opponents to aim down the alley if they wish, rather than playing the percentages by going down the middle. Yet be careful not to become *too* predictable in your zealousness to protect the middle. When the U.S. Davis Cup team of Jared Palmer and Jonathan Stark lost to Sweden's Jan Apell and Jonas Bjorkman in 1994, *Los Angeles Times* writer Julie Cart noted that "Palmer, in particular, telegraphed his intention to move away from the alley when Stark was receiving [serve], and the Swedes exploited the lines all day. It was part of the plan. 'We talked about that before the match,' Bjorkman said. 'We knew that they take a step in to get the volley. That's why we tried to go down the line.' "

Apparently neither U.S. player saw a problem with their positioning. "A good doubles team is trying to cut off the middle," Palmer said. "It's difficult when you are trying to cover the middle, which is the percentage play. They did a good job of rifling it down the line. They did exploit that."

Storm the Net at Every Opportunity

Always remember: The best teams are constantly moving forward, looking for every chance to gain control of the net. This is a game in which your team must learn — consciously and reflexively — to attack the net at every opportunity if your goal is at least an invitation to the Pismo Beach Open. The net is where you can win points quickly, as opposed to camping at the baseline, where a team must make fantastic shots and retrieves just to stay alive. In fact, the longer your team stays back when your opponents are at the net, the less chance you have to win the point. At best, playing deep against particularly aggressive teams, you must lob again and again — sometimes even on second service returns — to drive these players back, and even then you're fighting an uphill battle that is doomed to failure.

Rather than playing defensively like this, try to be equally aggressive and determined to take over the net yourselves. More specifically, as I stressed earlier in the book, when your team is serving, you and your partner should have one overriding goal in mind: Get to the net and control the net — together. And when you're receiving serve, your mission should be to steal the net away from the serving team by moving in behind a strong return.

Attack, not only because you'll get an

59 This is the view a player has when he's forced to hit from below the net tape. Not a pretty sight against opponents who are poised to capitalize on this opportunity for a putaway volley.

easier shot closer to the net, but because you'll unnerve the other team. For example, when your opponents are serving, they have the initial edge, but this advantage shifts if your team can come charging forward behind a well-placed return that forces the server to hit up from below net level. Suddenly, in fact, your team is poised to win the point.

Key Advice for Playing the Net

My recommended principles for playing the net begin with understanding that most club players fail to capitalize fully on their positioning up at the net, because they fail to move forward when they anticipate a drive or after they've volleyed. For whatever reasons (and I've discussed them in various parts of this book), too many players spectate in doubles when they're not directly involved in the point, instead of always being primed and up on their toes, thinking, "The next ball is coming to me!" Or they are so fearful of the lob that they fail to crowd the net for a potential putaway volley.

The following guidelines should help you become a force inside the service line.

1. Know who should take the shot. The player closer to the net has priority on any shot within reach. This axiom is clearly understood by an experi-

60 Notice how the player on the left has cut across the center line to take the volley because she is closer to the net than her partner.

enced team, where both players respond automatically, without hesitating.

Why? Well, a player who's close to the net can hit the ball at a sharp angle, sometimes 130 or 140 degrees, into an unguarded area of the court. Contrast this angle to the player volleying 10½ feet away from the net, who may have only a 30-degree hitting angle available into open court. Also, the chances of the ball coming back are greater if the player farther from the net hits it.

Moreover, if the player closer to the net hits down on the ball (which is the natural tendency on the volley, as opposed to taking a short swing through the ball), the result is usually not as catastrophic as when he hits from farther away. If he's on top of the net, he can hit a crummy volley and still win the point. But when a person must volley 15 to 20 feet back from the net, just the slightest downward hitting motion will send the ball into the net.

Unfortunately, applying my "closest to the net" advice to real-life situations sometimes leads to a giant argument that I've heard around the world, and it stems from this predominant belief: "This is my side and that's your side; DON'T GET ON MY SIDE!" Believing this to be an axiom of tennis doubles, one person gets mad at his partner, saying, "Hey, you stole my shot! You ran onto my side of the court, right in front of me!" And the partner, if he's wise to the game, answers, "You're right — but it was *my* shot; I was the closest person to the net, so if you want that shot, get your rear in gear."

If you find yourself complaining to a partner who's an apparent court hog in these volleying situations, you most likely are getting mad at the wrong person. Your partner (much to your good fortune, in most cases, unless he's disrupting your legitimate shot by coming onto your side of the court) is running in front of you to volley because he saw the drive coming and alertly broke forward, placing himself closer to the net and then "taking" your shot. So, instead of getting angry, just remember: You must earn your volleys by breaking forward and being the closest person to the net. There's no such thing as "my side, your side" in big-time tennis. It's zoom, zoom, crossing back and forth in front of one another. If a player is caught back, he wants his partner to jump across and take away his volley at the net.

One warning, however: When you cross the center stripe on the dead run, you now own that side, and your partner is obligated to take your side of the court. Don't cross the line and suddenly think, "Oh, oh, I shouldn't have gone," and then jump back, because you'll leave your partner in the lurch. You made a decision to go for the ball, and now you're responsible for hitting it.

If you're continually lagging your partner and tired of having her handle your case at the net, you must get out and practice. I used to play mixed doubles around Southern California with Louise Brough (5 times the Wimbledon doubles champ, 12 times the U.S. doubles winner), and she certainly wasn't shy about taking my volley if I took a medium approach to

A

B

61 A–B Up near the net, always be ready to break forward on a diagonal to intercept a ball on your partner's side of the court (A). Notice here how a fast-moving partner hits an easy volley from right on top of the net (B), saving his partner from a difficult low volley.

the ball. I still remember her saying, "Any time you're ready, Braden, come on up." I literally had to go out on an empty court before a match and practice my first step so that I could legitimately hold my own with Louise, a great woman and friend.

2. The best volleyer should cover shots down the middle. I've often noticed in club tennis that when a team is up at the net together, the person who takes every shot down the middle tends to have the biggest mouth. If it's a husband-and-wife team, whoever calls the shots in the family usually calls them on the court. But this "strategy" won't work well if you hope to develop a strong doubles team, nor does it help a typical marriage relationship.

Fortunately, there's an objective solution. If you and your partner are equally close to the net when the ball is hit, the player who has the better volley down the center should take the shot, be it a backhand or a forehand volley. It's not automatic that the forehand volleyer takes the shot, since some players actually have a better backhand volley than their partner's forehand volley. Ken Rosewall, for instance, had such a lethal backhand that you wouldn't have dreamt of getting in his way.

Try to resolve this down-the-middle decision early in the partnership, so that you minimize hesitation and on-court flare-ups. Too often, intermediates around the world are so indecisive or afraid to move that they both say "Yours!," and the ball passes between them, untouched and unharmed.

I like a $^5/_8$–$^3/_8$ system between two players. Once you and your partner agree upon who has the stronger volley down the middle, that player takes responsibility for $^5/_8$ of the distance between you, and it's clear he'll volley every ball that's coming dead center between you. This should help prevent a clashing of rackets as shots come up the middle and lead to more effective return volleys. Always remember, however, that the person with $^5/_8$ responsibility will proportionately make more errors, so the $^3/_8$ player must be patient and understanding.

The person who has priority should be thinking aggressively, always ready to move forward on a diagonal to hit an offensive shot. Where to aim? Back down the middle of the court, unless one opponent is slightly back and the other is slightly up, creating a diagonal between them that should be exploited. Or, aim for a weaker player's right hip (if he's right-handed; left hip for a left-hander) and force him to make a play.

A good team will develop automatic responses and should not be saying "Yours!," except at those rare times when a shot is right on the $^5/_8$–$^3/_8$ borderline. The better the team, the less you hear "Yours"; the weaker the team, the more you hear both partners calling it at the same time.

3. Crowd the net. The closer your team can approach the net, the more you can exploit the opposing team. As we've seen, you'll gain sharper angles for hitting putaway shots and you'll put more pressure on your opponents to execute, while opening up holes in their defense.

Against a drive (any shot that you can volley), this means your team must learn to get off the mark with a fast first step toward the net when you see a shot coming. Attack — don't wait for the ball to come to you. The ball drops rapidly, and if you let it sink below the tape of the net, you place yourself on the defensive and all you can do is try to punch the ball deep.

A

B

62 A–B Up at the net, both players should be poised for the attack, ready to break forward on a diagonal to cover the opponent's baseline drive.

63 The player in the foreground has made a tactical mistake. She sees that her opponent has to lift the ball defensively, but instead of getting up on her toes and leaning forward, ready to move in for a volley near the net, she has pulled up and is back on her heels.

Jack Kramer used to go nuts in the stands when he saw a player with good position hesitate and let the ball fall below the level of the net, then try to hit an offensive volley. Jack has seen few players in the history of the game who could take a low ball and convert it into an offensive volley with any real success.

Also, be sure to keep moving forward as you volley rather than stopping to admire your shot. This will help ensure sounder technique while advancing you even deeper for the next volley, if that opportunity arises. If your body is moving forward as you swing, your racket doesn't need to move as much, and this minimizes mis-hits; you can literally just position your racket and use your body momentum to supply the force.

4. Stay independently involved. Some players who have trouble in doubles are those who hero-worship their partner or who are dependent thinkers. They're always thinking, "My partner will get it." But if you want to help form a winning team, you must be ready for every situation that occurs. Your only thought should be, "I'm going to get the next ball." If your partner gets it, fine, but already you're anticipating the very next shot.

5. Learn to "read" your opponents' intentions. One reason many people fear

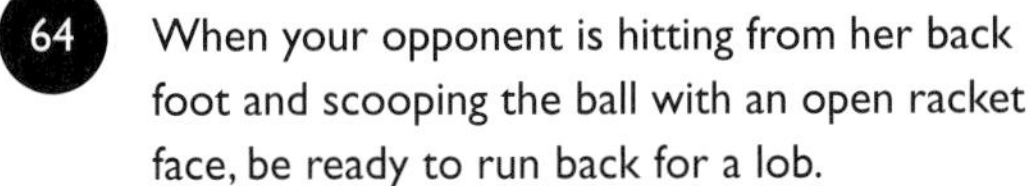

64 When your opponent is hitting from her back foot and scooping the ball with an open racket face, be ready to run back for a lob.

65 When your opponent has this look just before impact, she's not going to lob.

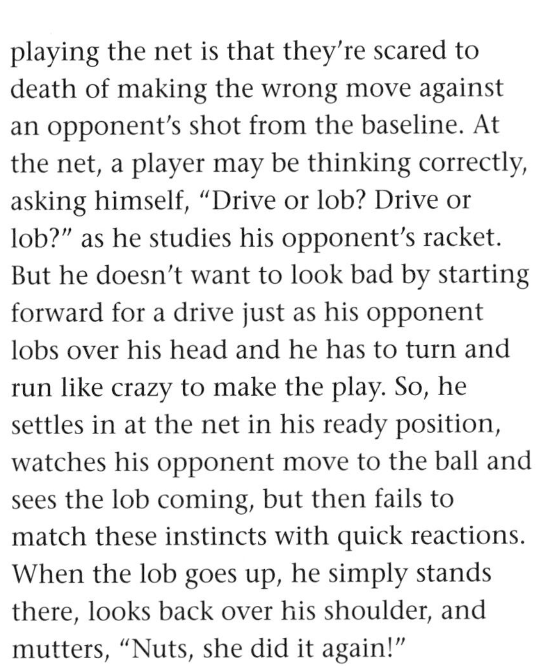

playing the net is that they're scared to death of making the wrong move against an opponent's shot from the baseline. At the net, a player may be thinking correctly, asking himself, "Drive or lob? Drive or lob?" as he studies his opponent's racket. But he doesn't want to look bad by starting forward for a drive just as his opponent lobs over his head and he has to turn and run like crazy to make the play. So, he settles in at the net in his ready position, watches his opponent move to the ball and sees the lob coming, but then fails to match these instincts with quick reactions. When the lob goes up, he simply stands there, looks back over his shoulder, and mutters, "Nuts, she did it again!"

To avoid shortchanging your team like this, start watching for the little tip-offs that reveal the kind of shot your opponent is going to hit — and then don't be afraid to react. Basically, study his racket and forearm as he swings into the ball. If he turns his forearm and the racket face opens up and tilts toward the sky, he's going to lob. If he swings level with a vertical racket face, he's going to drive the ball. Another clue is his footwork. If he leans back with his weight on the back foot, and his racket face has dropped low and is tilted back, he's going to lob; there's no way he can effectively drive the ball. But if he's stepping into the ball with his front foot, look for a drive.

Remember, too, that physical laws are at work on your behalf. We know from studies in motor-learning labs that once a person starts his swing and the racket is going forward, he cannot effectively change the motor programming; the brain has "fired" the program and there's no retrieving it. If he does try, he's caught in the middle between a drive and a lob, and the brain will be confused — trying to process two separate motor programs simultaneously — and this will lead to errors in execution.

Up at the net, deep down inside, you still may be thinking, "I know what Vic said, but this could be a trick." Fortunately it's too late for that to happen, which should give you the confidence to move instantly, knowing that once your opponent is committed to his swing, he can't change and try to fool you.

Defend Against the Lob

The question "Who takes the lobs?" is academic on a good team. When the ball goes over your heads, you and your partner should retreat together, each covering one-half of the court from the net to the baseline. Don't automatically turn around and say "Yours," because your partner may be saying the same thing.

It's wrong to assume, for example, that when your team is at the net and a lob goes over your partner's head on the right court, you should run back and try to make the play with your forehand. Each of you is responsible for a "sidewalk" that is exactly 18 feet wide and 39 feet long, unless one person for some reason is completely out of position (e.g., your partner has lunged to return a shot and hasn't recovered his balance) or is simply too slow at retreating.

Up at the net, if your team is always prepared to retreat for the ball and can trust individual instincts, you're going to take care of yourselves against lobs. The moment you see a lob coming, turn and run back three steps before looking up to see where the ball is. This will get you back quickly and still allow plenty of time to look up and begin tracking the ball's path. Try to avoid backpedaling, a slower, more constricted way to retreat that also tends to promote an awkward overhead hitting motion. When you can reach the service line before the ball reaches the net, nobody will ever lob over your head successfully. You will always be in a good position to lob, drive, or hit an overhead smash against the weak lob.

At my tennis college, I show students how they can cover virtually any lob if they just learn to "read" the shot coming and then turn and run hard toward the back fence, without looking up. They don't turn around until they hear the ball land, but they're stunned to realize how much time they have to return the lob (often with a retaliation lob, since smart opponents will have moved up to the net).

Once this realization sinks in, people start getting closer to the net for volleys, because they now have greater confidence about retreating for lobs. So their volleys also improve, without any change in hitting technique, because they have better positioning closer to the net. Before, their fear about their ability to move quickly backward to cover a lob was inhibiting their aggressiveness and causing them to play too far from the net, thereby undermining their volleys.

Here's another tip: When an opponent hits the first lob of the match too long, past the baseline, the next one is quite likely to come up short — presenting your team with an overhead opportunity. If you can put this shot away and win the point, you'll gain a psychological edge, since the opponent is now 0 for 2 with lobs, and that can be inhibiting for a less confident

66 Teammates should retreat quickly together to cover a lob by running versus backpedaling.

player. After hitting too long on the first lob of the match, his typical reaction will be, "Jeez, that's terrible; I've got to ease up." So he babies the next lob, and it comes up way too short. If your team can proceed to deck this easy overhead, you could have that opponent intimidated for the rest of the match.

Take Advantage of Your Own Lobs

A team that is continually lobbing is usually playing defensive doubles, but always remember: A good lob can take you quickly from the defensive to the offensive. In fact, if your opponents control the net, a deep lob from the baseline is normally the best percentage shot against intermediates, because so many players at this level have weak or inconsistent overheads and thus often fail to capitalize on a short lob. Against tournament 4.0/5.0-rated players, either a deep lob (diagonally, to gain more length) or a drive down the center of the court represents your best option. At the pro level, especially, where nearly every lob attempt results in a putaway overhead, most players think they have a better chance by driving the ball and hoping their opponents miss a volley. Reflecting the fact that it's tough to lob a great player in pro tennis because the overhead is such a great strength, Bobby Riggs told me in 1995 that he considered himself one of the greatest

A

B

67 A–B Remember the cardinal rule: The moment your team lobs successfully over your opponents' heads, match them step for step as they retreat and you move forward. The lobbing team in photo A has remained on the baseline and has thus squandered a great opportunity to gain control of the net. In photo B, they move up properly while their opponents make the mistake of backpedaling.

lobbers in the history of the game, yet he couldn't remember Jack Kramer ever missing an overhead against him.

When your opponents control the net and you lob the ball successfully over their heads, don't stand and watch them retreat. Move forward, matching them step for step, so that when they look around, whom should they see at the net? *Your team*. By closing in tightly on the net, 10 to 12 feet apart, you'll allow your opponents only the barest of openings for a passing shot.

Keeping in mind my advice when defending against an opponent's lob ("If the first one in the match goes long, the next one will likely come up short"), when you're practicing lobs before a match and the ball is going long, don't alter your swing. Instead, simply hit the ball higher in the air with the same speed, and it should land inside the baseline. As the hitter, if your lob goes long, think about it as a good lob, knowing that you must now just hit the next one higher but at the same speed and it should fall inside the baseline. This should keep you from falling into the "one deep, one short" syndrome.

Decide Who Has Priority on the Overhead

When there's time for either partner to hit the overhead, who has priority? Bottom line: The person who can put the ball away best — under pressure — should take the shot, even if this means shifting court positions from left to right or right to left. If your individual putaway abilities are about equal, each player should take the overheads that travel to his or her side of the court.

These decisions should be worked out before a match and as your partnership gains experience. Unfortunately, some teams have trouble reaching an agreement here, especially in mixed doubles, where often I hear the woman partner complain, "My overhead is just as good as my partner's, but he always crowds me out and tries to hit every one. What can I do?"

My advice here is this: If you can't convince a ball-hog partner that your overhead is as good as his, ask a friend or the club pro to hit 20 lobs to each of you and have that person judge who's better at putting the ball away. The person doing this evaluation should try to return each overhead so that he has a realistic sense of just how effective the two of you are — with the emphasis on placement rather than speed. If he determines that you indeed have a more lethal overhead, it's now your partner's responsibility to back off and let you dictate the shot at every opportunity. Of course, if your overhead is actually less impressive than you thought, be prepared to let your partner hit the in-between opportunities.

Poach

Poaching is a tactic that should be incorporated into your team's strategy not just on the serve but also at key times once the point is under way, when you sense that your opponent is going to hit the ball crosscourt and you cut to the middle — on a forward diagonal — just as he's contacting the ball, when he can't change his mind and go down the line. If you can break at the right time and move into the net (while, of course, anticipating the crosscourt shot), few shots will ever get past you.

The only downside to poaching that I've

seen is that the poacher may take off too early or too late, but that's an easily corrected problem. What counts here is that opponents tend to hit a lot of crummy shots when they have to worry about your team's poaching throughout a match, and people often forget just how many points a good poacher wins, never having touched the ball. Even partners sometimes overlook this virtue when they get upset after their poaching partner misses an easy volley.

Once the point begins, the key to poaching is for the player closer to the net to understand that he "owns" the net from net post to net post, and he should never feel inhibited about moving into his partner's territory to take a shot. If you have position on your partner and you sense, for example, that an opponent is going to hit his favorite crosscourt shot — but you're in a down-the-line position — you should feel free to break across and poach. "Guess" right and you'll invariably have a putaway volley opportunity. Meanwhile, of course, your partner must be ready to cover the territory you have abandoned, just in case you have misread your opponent's intentions.

After the point is under way, top players have an instinctive understanding with their partner that goes basically like this: "If you're back and I'm up, and the opponent's deep in the corner, look for me to go and be ready to cover my side." In fact, the goal in good doubles is to be so well in sync with one's partner that visual signals are unnecessary because you know what each person is going to do in most circumstances.

Start practicing more poaching as you play your matches and notice how many more balls you get to hit up at the net, and how much more fun you have.

Use the Short Ball as a Weapon

Try to concentrate early in the match on how well your opponents handle short balls that draw them in from the baseline or as they attack. This will help you determine how aggressive you should be about capitalizing on one of the basic tactics in good doubles: When you hit the ball short, either deliberately or in error, move forward — don't hang back. Many players have trouble returning a short ball or hate to move up into short-ball territory, fearful they are going to have to hit a low volley. These opponents should be attacked, because they invariably catch the net or lift the ball high with their return shot, presenting putaway volley opportunities. Two-handed players, in particular, are vulnerable to the well-placed short ball.

Against a short ball, not only is your opponent having to bend down and stretch out for a shot he doesn't like in the first place, there's also the element of distraction as he sees you charging in. Ken Rosewall moved in behind a short ball as well as anyone I've ever seen, and Gigi Fernandez does it well among today's players. Remember again that from a motor-learning standpoint, the more variables you can place in an opponent's head, the more apt he is to recruit the wrong muscles when he goes to swing.

Capitalize on a Team's Weak Links

Clever gamesmanship in doubles (within sportsmanship boundaries) can often help an experienced team upset a stronger but less savvy team. Yet I must say that I've never met a great team that discussed "gamesmanship." Every conversation I've overheard in this regard was relative to

A B C D

68 A–D When the serving team poaches, the player at the net waits for the ball to pass (B), then breaks into the middle to volley the anticipated return (C). Meanwhile, the server breaks over to cover his vacated side of the court (D).

A

B

69 A–B When a player bends low to hit a half-volley (A), he must lift the ball to keep it out of the net, which usually produces an easy, high volley for the player who crowds the net (B). Although this player is in trouble, his racket face is angled down, and he will probably hit the lowest shot possible.

tennis facts, for example, "She's slow moving to the left," or "We can attack his second serve." I can't remember hearing players say, "Let's see if we can drive them nuts by grunting on every shot," although I have seen a lot of mediocre teams trying bizarre tactics. Also, I tell everyone that they should smile when they see gamesmanship moves because it often means that the opponents are beginning to worry and they feel they need something besides their faltering strokes to win.

Still, here are some suggested tactics that can help you legitimately exploit an opposing team without necessarily provoking a fistfight or a lawsuit.

1. Let's say you're playing a team that has a player who is particularly short. When he's in the backcourt, try to keep him pinned back there by hitting looping topspin shots. The high-bounding balls will force him to make contact at a high and undesired level. If he tries to retreat beyond the baseline to play the shots at normal height, he may find himself bouncing off the fence.

2. If an opponent is exceptionally tall, try to hit a lot of shots with soft underspin, which helps keep the ball low and forces him to bend down. It's not easy for a tall player to continually stretch out for low volleys. Not only does a low-bounding shot

hasten his fatigue, it demands that he lift the ball in order to clear the net, allowing you and your partner to move in for the kill.

3. Another good time to emphasize underspin is when your opponents are especially slow moving. When you can chip the ball toward open areas on the court, it will stay low once it hits the court, and lead-footed opponents may have to call a cab to reach it in time.

4. If you know that one of your opponents is particularly loath to go to the net, use underspin shots to bring her in from the baseline, and then — if the opportunity arises — hit the ball right at her and challenge her volleying ability.

5. Don't be afraid to attack the weaker or most vulnerable opponent (unless you're just playing social doubles). This person is fair game in league and tournament doubles, and if he or she is coming to the net or playing close to the net, the place you want to aim (against a right-hander) is the right hip. If the player complains, "You tried to hit me!" you should reply, "Yes — in the right hip." This is a handcuffing type of shot, almost physiologically impossible to volley on short notice. (Of course, the understanding here is that your intent is not to hurt this person, but to win the point. Moreover, you should go for the hip only when a wide — and safer — opening is not available. Now if an opponent is up at the net and tries to distract you by challenging your putaway overhead instead of turning his back or quickly retreating, this is unsportsmanlike conduct and he deserves getting hit by the ball. As angry as he might get, remember: He's unfairly trying to control your game by asking you to only play shots around him, even if it causes you to make an error or hit a retrievable shot toward his partner.)

Also, when you're playing mixed doubles and you happen to hit the woman in the chest — or you're the woman who gets hit in the chest — remember that this is acceptable gamesmanship in most tennis circles. Even that gentleman pro Arthur Ashe suggested this strategy for mixed doubles, saying: "If you're going to play to win, the first thing the man really wants to do is intimidate the other woman if she can be intimidated. You can't intimidate Margaret Court or Evonne [Goolagong] or Virginia Wade, but some of the lesser girls, you certainly can intimidate them. All you do is hit them in the chest if you can and they back off."

Arthur had a warm and friendly tone as he gave this advice to a woman at one of his clinics, and it still holds true.

6. You'll find that some doubles teams are great as long as they can play in a comfortable, familiar groove, but often begin playing like toads when suddenly confronted by new things that are thrown at them. Mix things up, by poaching and by hitting an occasional unpredictable shot, so that you keep your opponents as off-balanced as possible. Plant doubt in your opponents and they may begin to doubt themselves.

For example, even if your opponent "reads" your poaching intentions early, she could be so distracted that she misses her shot. Or, you might poach and miss your own shot two or three times early in the match; but that constant threat of poaching, whether on the serve or once the rally is under way, will still worry your opponents and should eventually work to your advantage. When you can poach effectively, you can easily manipulate people mentally as you break for the ball, or even just by faking with a shoulder movement or a little knee action. The great Australian doubles player Freddie McNair once told me, "If my partner is serving and I poach on the first ball and my opponents hit down the line and win the point, I guarantee you I'm poaching on the very next serve. I'm not going to let them think they can put me in a slot and keep me there."

7. The longer your team plays together, the more you will discover how you can manipulate, and literally control, a team that has better players but poor teamwork.

For example, you really can take advantage of a team that fails to move in tandem and gets together only when they shake hands at the end of a match. If one player runs back for a lob and his partner stays up at the net, you've been given a gaping opening for your next shot. Similarly, if one opponent runs way out of court and his partner fails to shift over with him, be ready to exploit that subsequent hole up the middle.

Remember, too, that sometimes just unexpected movement alone is enough to disrupt another team. Most people who play doubles have a set formula and they know what to expect from their regular opponents. Then they enter a tournament and come up against a team that's moving all the time, poaching and crisscrossing back and forth, and it flusters them because there are too many things going on.

Have a "Last-Resort" Strategy

I'm sometimes asked, "At what point does it actually pay to guess in doubles?" And my answer is, "When you're down 5–40 or love–40." Statistically, your chances of eventually winning the game are better if you start guessing here as to where your opponents are going to hit, and poach in that direction, than if you simply stay in the same place, undecided about which direction to break, until the ball is actually hit.

Scout the Other Team

I've always felt that a surprising number of doubles matches could be won from the fourth row of the bleachers by an observant doubles team that takes time to scout potential opponents — around the club, in team tennis, or at a tournament. When you and your partner can study other teams together, I think you'll find that you gain valuable insights that improve your prematch preparations, enhance your sense of teamwork, and strengthen your team's performance.

One reason I've been such an advocate of scouting over the years is that every player has predictable patterns in shot selection and execution — right out there for everyone to see — and you can trust these probabilities to keep occurring throughout a match. If a person has a favorite shot to a particular part of the court, you can bet the house that he's going to stick with it under pressure, because shot-making flexibility and surprise are weak points with most players. Nearly everybody develops a certain motor program in tennis — a "software package" — and under stress, that package keeps coming back. That's where you can capitalize on scouting. (Bill Jacobson of CompuTennis, through shot-by-shot computer analysis of entire matches, has

70 An aggressive team can be deadly when volleying from close to the net against a team that has one player up and one player back.

found that certain players will almost invariably hit a certain shot when they're in a certain jam, 90 or 95 percent of the time. If you can log this kind of data about a particular opponent, in a notebook, for example, obviously you gain a big-time advantage in anticipation alone.)

When I'm working with a student and trying to improve a particular technique, he often responds, "Vic, I know it's better to hit this way when I'm out there in a match, but the moment I get under pressure, I revert to my old game." Well, let that candid admission provide a lesson. When most players are under pressure, they revert to their comfortable stroking habits and favorable shots, so if you know what a player's grooved preferences are, you can capitalize on that knowledge when you play that person in doubles.

During a tournament, or just around the club on a busy weekend, you and your partner should take advantage of the inevitable waiting time to scout potential future opponents. Write down your observations in a notebook so that you later have a clear idea about how you can devise tactics based more accurately upon a team's skills and style of play. Knowing how probable it is that your opponents will choose to hit a particular shot in a pressure situation will not necessarily enable you to win a tremendous number of points, but it should pay off on the key points as you draw on your homework.

As you scout a potential team, here are some points you should analyze:

- How well do they get their first serves in play?
- Can their second serves be attacked?
- Do they follow their serves to the net?
- When each player serves and attacks, how deep does that player get for his volley? And how effectively does he volley at various heights?
- How well do they place overheads, and where do they usually hit them?
- How effective are their overheads from midcourt compared to their overheads from around the baseline?
- How well do they lob from each side? Does one player always lob short from his backhand side?
- How are their lobs from a relatively stationary position from behind the baseline compared to their lobs while desperately retrieving?
- How well do they cover deep lobs? Do they each cover their own side of the court or does one player do all the work?
- How well (low or high) do they hit service returns?
- How effective are they at returning serve away from the net player and at the feet of the onrushing server?
- Can they handle a good slice serve? Kick serve?
- Are they so predictable that an Australian formation could confuse them?
- How strong are their forehand ground strokes?
- Do they have effective backhand ground strokes?
- Do they concentrate on hitting down the middle? Or do they often aim down the line, even when a good opening isn't there?
- Do they clearly reveal their intention to drive or lob?
- How well do they cover lobs?
- Are they vulnerable to an offensive lob because they crowd too close to the net?
- Are their high volleys crisp and accurate?
- Are they good at hitting low volleys? What about half-volleys?
- How are they at hitting volleys from midcourt?
- Are they fast afoot, and how willing are they to attack the net?

- How well do they move as a team in response to the ball? Do they seem to anticipate shots well?
- Are they in shape?
- Do they seem to fear fast action?
- Do they have fast hands for quick exchanges at the net?
- Do they poach on the serve, and are they deceptive?
- Do they poach at any time after the point is under way? How effectively do they seem to anticipate their opponent's shot?
- Do they have a tendency to poach from a particular side?
- Do they have trends on big points?
- Do they seem to play better and harder when the set is on the line either way?
- Do they have a tendency to get down on themselves?
- Do they communicate and give each other support?

When studying another team from the sidelines, be careful not to base everything on how well they execute just two or three particular shots, since this can prove misleading.

For example, people have a tendency to be overly impressed by the way a particular team poaches at the net and to think, "They're dynamite." But maybe that team looks great poaching simply because their opponents have been hitting weak service returns that set up the poach. Or maybe their opponents are far too predictable as to where they hit the ball. What counts is what happens when they're pressed by a good team — not only on the serve, but during a rally. Also, don't be so enamored with their poaching that you fail to analyze how well they hit overheads and how well they volley low balls at their feet, and other plays like that. They may love to poach, but can they follow up with the right shots — especially if your team responds with a strong attack?

We tend to fixate on someone's best shot and evaluate that person's whole game based on that best shot. So create a checklist and then study your answers carefully.

Eventually, as you gain experience playing with a regular partner, playing doubles ought to feel like you're emulating a tightly held Blue Angels formation, swooping across the court. When your team plays a textbook point — executing your first shot properly, moving as a team, and closing off the point with a killer volley — there's hardly a better feeling in tennis.

CHAPTER 7

Key Individual Shots in Doubles

THE irony of doubles is that while you are playing with a partner and sharing the responsibility as a team, you must have the individual shots necessary to win points and keep your team alive. Every stroke from singles has value in doubles, but as I've stressed, the serve, service return, and volley are of particular importance. Let's explore these strokes from a doubles perspective, in terms of execution and tactics. (See also chap. 9, where I talk about improvement.)

The Slice Serve

In doubles and singles alike, the hard, sliced serve is the most overlooked, underused weapon in tennis today. This serve (when hit by a right-hander into the deuce court) travels from right to left and stays low after striking the court, forcing the opponent toward the side fence. The best he can do is lob the ball deep on a diagonal, or try to drive the return down the line as he prays — quite appropriately — for a miracle.

Few club players can actually run an opponent into the side fence with a slice ("spin") serve, but sufficient skill can be acquired with attention to the right technique. The resulting shot can help you capitalize on an opponent's positioning and stroking weaknesses in a number of ways.

1. If he's overplaying the backhand side by standing close to the center stripe in his ready position, he's vulnerable to a serve hit wide to his forehand. Even though he may have a powerful forehand, few players can run wide for a ball like this and return it offensively, so your opponent is on the defensive as you come to the net. If he tries

71 A–D This player practices his slice serve against an opponent. The ball is tossed on the right side (A), which allows him to move further forward on the hit while protecting his options to hit a slice or flat serve. His forearm is pronating to the right, which generates speed as he contacts the ball (B). From a slightly different angle, notice how the racket appears to be on edge as he imparts sidespin on the ball (C). He then practices following his shot to the net (D).

72 A–C The server is planning to slice the ball wide to his opponent's forehand (A). His partner knows this and is prepared for a down-the-line return (often the only return against a good slice serve). The slice serve is perfect, and the opponent returns down the line, but the server's partner is already moving to the anticipated shot (B), and he easily hits his volley to the huge opening between his opponents (C).

A

B

C

to go down the line, he must aim down a narrow lane while on the run, and your partner is there to volley the return — most likely back toward his weak backhand side. (Of course, a poorly executed slice, hit with too little sidespin, will easily undermine your devious intentions. Your serve will fail to move your opponent far enough off the court to cause him trouble, and the ball will have a more horizontal bounce when it hits, thus giving him an easier return to pound with his big forehand — and creating real pressure on your partner up at the net.)

2. Since the slice serve has a lower trajectory than one hit with topspin, it bounces lower and can be particularly effective against a tall player who hates to bend down and stretch out, or against anybody who has slow lateral movement.

3. Taking a little pace off the serve allows you to get closer to the net without handing your opponent an easier serve to return. By staying low after it bounces, a sliced serve forces your opponent to raise his return, giving you a potentially easier ball to volley as you move in.

4. Slicing the serve wide can create gaps in the other team's court coverage. You

separate your opponents, opening up the middle between them, unless the netman moves over to help compensate for his partner's moving off-court. If he does, that leaves his team vulnerable to his back side, down the line.

5. I like a slice's element of surprise (when intentions are successfully camouflaged) and the fact that most players are uncomfortable at best when forced to return serve throughout the match from beyond the doubles sidelines. They are highly anxious when they face this prospect, obviously preferring to stay between the lines, covering serves with three steps to the left or three steps to the right and then stepping into the ball as they hit.

6. When the returner is forced wide, he's often tempted to go for a down-the-line "winner," which is exactly what you want. Hitting from here (as photos 73 A–B show), his diagonal return must travel most of the distance out of the court, toward a tiny target area that nobody can consistently hit. The receiver's alternative is to attempt to return the ball on a hard, sharp angle toward center court. But that's a difficult challenge for him if you're coming in behind your serve, since you're cutting off the angle and can easily intercept the ball. Meanwhile, your partner at the net can simply overplay your side, knowing that the returner will be lucky to reach the ball, let alone be able to hit a return that hurts your team. Even the pros can do no better than land the ball near midcourt on returns — right where the server should be as he rushes the net.

A

B

73 A–B When the server (here, a left-hander) can drive the receiver off the court with a slice serve, notice how foolhardy it is for the receiver to attempt to return the ball down the line into the back corner (A). This requires one of the most precise shots in tennis, for the ball must travel a path that is out of court virtually the entire distance. In order to keep the ball away from the partner of the server (player 1), the receiver has to hit a target area of about two square feet. There's not a player alive who can pull this shot off consistently, which is why the receiver should instead either lob or try to drive the ball crosscourt.

Hitting Technique

Since most players, except those at the pro level, tip off their intentions of hitting a big slice by tossing the ball way off to the side, remember this: Just a normal toss is needed, to the same location that you toss the ball for your "flat" serve (but about 8 to 10 inches to the right of your topspin serve toss).

What counts is that you (1) contact the ball well out in front of your body so that you can (2) brush the center of the back right side of the ball as the racket moves across on an almost horizontal plane to produce sidespin.

Also make sure that your service motion looks the same as your other serves, so that your opponents can't read the shot coming. Contacting the ball out ahead of your body allows you to step slightly to the right and hit further outside the ball, resulting in a better slice without giving away your intentions — providing you throw the ball to the same place on the toss.

Years ago Jack Kramer was a master of the hard, sliced serve, and it was one of the key strokes in his arsenal. If he was hitting hard and flat (as he preferred), but his opponent was starting to groove in, then he would suddenly slice the ball — contacting it way out in front of his body — and force his opponent well off the court. Most pro-tournament courts are 75 feet wide or more, but on a typical 60-foot-wide club court, Jack could hit the side fence with the ball before it reached the baseline.

Arthur Ashe also had a tough slice to handle; and he went a long way with the shot, along with John McEnroe, whose left-handed slice from the ad court would invariably push the returner well outside the doubles alley and helped him win seven Grand Slam doubles titles with Peter Fleming.

Yet, to my amazement, I haven't seen one other player come along in pro tennis who has really worked hard on perfecting this particular serve. In the women's game, for example, opponents continually serve the ball straight at Steffi Graf, and she continually busts the return. Nobody is driving her off the court with a slice. Meanwhile, in men's pro tennis and wherever players are hitting the ball hard and taking it on the rise at the baseline, the slice serve could become more important than ever. Why? Well, research shows that if a Monica Seles takes the ball on the rise, it isn't that she hits the ball harder, it's that her shot returns more quickly and thus reduces her opponent's response time by 50 percent. But if the server can move this type of player laterally with a slice serve, that player can't cut the ball off so easily and take it on the rise, thus giving the server more time to move into the net.

Why don't the pros spend time working on a good slice serve? One reason is that they're obsessed with speed; they truly believe that a fast serve is the most important aspect of this stroke. A 110-m.p.h. serve is certainly a gigantic weapon, yet when the receiver can "read" the serve and reach his hitting position, that same speed becomes a weakness for the server. In reality, speed — straight at a person — is not that hard to handle; and the ball comes back faster to the server, so he's further back when he tries to attack the net; he's forced to volley from a deeper position.

Also, while some pros are pretty arrogant about their technique, down inside they're scared to make changes. They may be unhappy about their present ranking, dissatisfied at their lack of progress, but they're afraid if they throw everything into mastering an element like the slice serve, this will somehow undermine other aspects of their serve and cause them to backslide. I've seen this fear persist in several pros even after we've experimented together on the practice court with some new aspect of their serve and they've experienced the potential results and what this improvement could mean to their game.

The Volley

Since the most important strategy in doubles is to gain the net and maintain control of that fortress, let's scrutinize the volleying skills, both mental and physical, that are critical for capitalizing on these goals.

Quite possibly your critical breakthrough to make as a volleyer is to overcome fears of getting a "fuzz sandwich" up at the net — particularly in doubles, where opponents are closer to one another when they hit and there's less reaction time. People are reluctant to admit these qualms, but the problem certainly exists, especially for women in cutthroat mixed doubles.

The main problem with fear, aside from ruining some of the fun you should be having playing doubles, is that it inhibits movement and undermines the confidence and aggressiveness needed to be an effective volleyer. Boldness frees you to move offensively toward the ball — ideally, on a forward diagonal, so that you're moving into the shot and making contact out in front of your body.

If you have palpitations at the net, afraid that you're going to get nailed by a hostile opponent, there's a potential solution — but it's hard to wear a baseball batting helmet on court and not feel a bit ridiculous. So what to do?

Well, people tell me that playing with an oversized racket seems to ease their anxieties a bit, which in turn leads to faster reactions and quicker footwork. But the

A

B

74 A–B The player at the net anticipates the down-the-line shot before his opponent strikes the ball (A), and he can easily reach any ball hit down the alley (B). In fact, a player who can react before the ball is struck can cover three steps at the net in either direction.

best way to remove this element of fear and gain confidence at the net is to learn how to volley and defend yourself. When my students discover they can get out of the way of the ball by moving into the ball to hit faster than they can move sideways or back away from the ball, they gain the confidence to go forward in an aggressive manner.

What counts is not to be inhibited by what you may perceive as physical limitations in your game. Even strong doubles players often don't realize they can get two steps forward on most volleys. When I stress how important this is, they respond, "Yeah, but that's for the pros." Actually, it's the reverse. The pros hit the ball so hard, they make it difficult for their opponents to get two steps. But at the intermediate level, a player who knows how important it is to move forward to volley with a fast first step can often get three steps to the ball, which makes him lethal when he volleys. Also remember: The closer you can get to the net, the less talent you need to hit a winning volley.

When it comes to execution, pay attention to physicist Howard Brody's data on gravity trajectories as they relate to hitting a hard, flat volley from above net level. He shows that if you move in on the ball with your hitting elbow up and the racket face vertical, it's almost impossible to knock the ball out, no matter how hard you hit it (providing you don't turn the bottom of the racket under at impact). Nearly everyone says, "My God, if I hit a volley that hard, it'll strike the back fence." But it doesn't work that way, thanks to gravity.

On the Brody scale, against a ball traveling 80 m.p.h., if you stand one foot behind the service line and volley the ball from a four-foot height on a horizontal plane (swinging straight across with the racket face straight up and down at impact), the ball just clears the net by five inches and lands eight feet inside the baseline. It cannot go out, at sea level, because of gravity. This means that one can crunch the ball on a horizontal plane and the ball still lands in, so don't hit down on volleys!

Unfortunately, most beginners and intermediates are afraid to volley this hard. They tend to come in and baby the ball when they're close to the net, and if their shot does indeed stay in play — rather than go into the net — it usually falls short and provides an easy return for the opponents.

Hitting Technique

Of course, it takes the right technique to volley aggressively the way I recommend. Here are some tips to help make you a feared and respected volleyer.

1. On all volleys, whether you're contacting the ball at knee level or above eye level, try to master a short, punching motion rather than an actual stroke, because the greater the length of your swing, the greater must be your talent. Some pros literally fix their rackets in a position and move their body through the shot for their power.

2. Hit through the ball and finish with your racket at eye level. This helps ensure a desired stroking pattern — forward to the target, not down — as your racket comes through the hitting zone. Finishing high with the racket also leaves you ready for a follow-up volley as you move to the net. In contrast, when you swing down to impart underspin, the racket face has to be tilted to compensate, and the calculations are severe.

A

75 A–C Moving aggressively to the ball, this player has the right idea on the backhand volley. He takes a short backswing (controlled by the non-hitting hand) and volleys from the shoulder (A), letting his body provide the power, so that his swing can be short and accurate. Notice how his eyes are focused on the ball (B) and that his follow-through remains high with no forearm movement as he closes in on the net for a possible follow-up shot (C).

B

C

A

B

C

76 A–C As the hitter moves forward to hit an underspin approach shot, notice how the backswing is short (A), the stroke is slightly down on a severe incoming angle (B), and the follow-through is high and he's ready for the next shot (C).

3. Keep the hitting elbow up as you swing, so that the racket face can be vertical at impact. If the elbow stays in near your body, the racket will lie back, which is what you want to avoid. Over the years, I've emphasized more and more the crucial importance of keeping the elbow up and volleying from the shoulder. John McEnroe mastered this so well. With the elbow up, you only have to turn your body and volley from the shoulder instead of the forearm, and if the racket's perfect, you can hit the heck out of the volley and have a hard time hitting it out. But if you rely on forearm action, the racket will be dragging, which leads to trouble.

4. Avoid facing the net as you volley. Instead, try to be turned sideways as often as possible in order to volley sharply and minimize the times you pull down on the ball. The slightest downswing will kill your shot, especially when there's a quick exchange of volleys. If you insist on facing the net, notice how difficult it is to go out to meet the ball and to come across an imaginary shelf as you swing.

77 A–C Here the player demonstrates the forearm-only volley and the unfortunate results it often produces. The racket head must be timed to meet the ball perfectly with the correct racket-face opening, or the ball either drops into the net (C) or falls quite short in the opponents' court.

A

B

C

5. Know your volley "window" over the net. When you visualize a target area that is safely above the net rather than on the opposite court, and consciously try to hit through that window, the ball tends to stay clear of the net.

6. Also, strive to have your racket, your eyes, and the ball all on the same level at contact. If the ball comes over low, bend down in order to position the racket correctly to get your shot up and over the net. But avoid trying to hit a low-percentage, sharply angled volley (unless your opponents are both deep). Instead, play the shot defensively and aim deep to your opponents' baseline if possible.

7. Motor programming can help you respond to close-quarter exchanges and minimize the times you swing down on the ball and catch the net. The required reactions and movements are so fast here that the brain doesn't have time to consciously program an effective muscular response. But you can certainly preprogram your thinking — "hit out, not down" — so that whatever the circumstances and pressure,

78 When you're coming in for a low volley, get low to the ball so that you have more control and consistency hitting this shot. If you're going to play a serve-and-volley game, work on your leg strength because you're going to be forced into shots like this all match long.

79 In this close-quarter exchange, the key is to have quick reactions and a short, crisp volley stroke from both sides.

your hitting motion is automatic and the racket head stays high through impact.

8. When you receive a crosscourt ground stroke and you intend to volley down the line, you must swing aggressively and crunch the ball in order to counteract the angle of deflection and keep the ball in play. Many players make a big mistake here by holding the racket still and barely striking the ball, thinking this is all they have to do to hit a sure-fire winner. Alas, the ball invariably deflects out of play, traveling wide of the alley.

9. In doubles especially, just getting the ball back won't win many points — you must volley aggressively to put opponents on the defensive or to slip the ball through openings in their defense.

Movement Tips

Ingraining some key mental factors and movement skills can help you win points with your volley simply by allowing you to reach the ball earlier and get closer to the net. The sooner you contact the ball, the higher above the net you can volley — making for an easier, safer shot. And the closer you approach the net, the greater your potential hitting angles.

- Instead of standing and waiting for the crowd to cheer, run through the volley as you hit, always trying to advance closer to the net for your next shot. Forward momentum will enable you to crowd the net for a follow-up volley.
- Whenever you sense the opportunity, trust your instincts and break quickly forward on a diagonal toward the ball. Here's where your ability to get a fast first step is so important.

The Overhead

The overhead is a putaway shot we work hard to get, yet one even the pros still "choke" on occasion by knocking the ball into the back fence or down into the net. Clearly, this is not a cinch shot. For one thing, you're hitting a ball that is falling from a greater height and at a faster speed than your service toss (which, ideally, should be contacted at or near its peak). Thus, your timing in the hitting zone is critical, for you have only an instant to contact the ball at a desired point.

The most common error on the overhead is to forget the "Eight Degree Rule" as devised by physicist Pat Keating (for a typical lob, which is normally falling at about a 45-degree angle when struck). He has shown that instead of hitting down on the ball from near the midcourt area, you actually must swing forward and up, at about an eight-degree angle, in order to counteract the physics at work. The ball is falling, and you must get forward and counteract the incoming angle at impact. This will help keep the ball out of the net and send it deep or well-angled toward an alley. (It is important to remember here that the racket head is perpendicular to the court — straight up and down — and going up at about an eight-degree angle, not laid back eight degrees. Also, you can certainly hit down on the overhead when you're up at the net.)

In order to contact the ball properly with an upward force, good preparation is critical. Keep your feet moving as you try to get into a comfortable hitting position as early as possible. Be aggressive and don't wait for the ball to come to you, because you must hit *up* at this falling ball, not down (unless you're right on top of the

80 This player practices with a pro, receiving severe crosscourt shots and measuring her target. If she simply holds her racket head still, she must aim for the center of the baseline to have her shot go into the backhand corner. If she has slow movement forward with her racket, she will aim halfway between the center mark and the backhand corner. And if she has a pretty aggressive movement with her racket on the volley, she will aim about three feet inside the corner.

81 These three players illustrate how important it is to move in tight on the net. Against a crosscourt passing shot, the player in front can volley that shot by taking just one step to his left. Player 2 has to take two steps, and player 3, back near the service line, is three steps away from the shot and thus, obviously, more vulnerable to a crosscourt shot.

A B

82 A–B The player in photo A is guilty of a common error on the overhead — pointing to the ball as it falls. Instead, she should "point" with a bent elbow, which facilitates coiling the body and producing more power and rhythm in the swing (B).

net). Even a short, weak lob demands nimble footwork, proper positioning, and attention to good stroking technique. If you get careless, all too often the ball will end up falling too close to your head or too low out in front.

When self-evaluating your technique, make sure you're swinging with a loose throwing motion, just as I teach on the serve. One way to help ensure this uncoiling action by the body is to avoid pointing your finger too early at the ball as it comes your way, since early "finger-pointing" stiffens the body and inhibits the upper-body rotation you seek. Instead, rotate your non-hitting shoulder away from the net and then track the incoming ball with a bent left elbow or your finger, in the natural sequence of the body unwinding. One reason Monica Seles has one of the best overhead smashes in tennis is that she coils her body as she prepares to hit and doesn't point her finger as she tracks the ball.

Just as on the serve, another way to safeguard your overhead is to tell yourself, "Keep your chin up" — with your head extremely still — as you swing. Also, consciously think about keeping your front shoulder going up in the direction of the ball as you coil on a horizontal, so that your head and upper body don't collapse before impact.

Whatever your psychological makeup and overhead ability, always try to "deck" every overhead opportunity, hard and deep, but without being reckless. You'll miss an occasional overhead hitting aggressively like this, but your opponents will feel the heat and should be far less inclined to send up lobs when they're in trouble — thus forsaking the one shot that can give them a reprieve and force your team back from the net. When you ease off on the overhead, happy to keep the rally alive or trying to play it safe by aiming for the midcourt area, you simply give the other team an incentive to keep lobbing when they're in trouble, knowing that they rarely will have to pay the price for a high but short lob.

Also, don't be scared off by the fact you might accidentally hit one of your opponents. That's just part of the game. Nor should you let a hot dog opponent try to distract you or force you to aim in another direction by standing right in front and waving his racket as you wind up to smash an overhead. It's his responsibility to get out of the way or to turn his back as a sign of submission, basically conceding the point. If he turns away, try to hit a clean winner away from his body without risking your shot, but if you still happen to hit him, good etiquette dictates that you raise your hand and apologize. If your hand isn't up when he turns around, then it's war — and the next time he has an overhead near the net, your smartest move will be to run in the opposite direction. (You should be rightfully irritated by the opponent who tries to stand in your way when you get an overhead smash. This person wants two for two: He wants to distract you into missing the shot and he wants to make sure you miss him. Well, that's unsportsmanlike conduct, and if he insists upon putting himself in a vulnerable position, he has to accept the fact that he may get a "fuzz sandwich" — or, even worse, a detached retina.)

Another safety reminder: When your partner is behind you and preparing to hit an overhead smash, don't turn around to watch him swing. He may mishit and give you a new look. Besides, you'll know exactly where your partner is hitting by watching your opponents, and you'll be able to respond and move faster to a return shot than you would by watching your partner and then turning.

The Lob

The lowly lob, hit with either offensive or defensive intent, is perhaps the most neglected shot during fast-paced doubles rallies, when it should be viewed as a critical weapon at any level of play. You may snicker or look disdainfully upon a team that sends up a helium ball at every opportunity, but when both players can lob effectively, they very likely have more doubles trophies at home than anyone else at your club. That's because the well-timed, well-executed lob can provide a number of advantages — especially when the other team is weak on overheads.

1. When hit high and deep, the lob can bail you out of trouble by allowing your

83 When you're scrambling and the other team controls the net, throw up a lob, as the left-hander is doing here.

84 When forced back behind the baseline, try to regain control of the net by lobbing deep and moving quickly forward with your partner as your opponents retreat.

team to "buy time" to recover and stay in the point after scrambling off-court.

2. It can disrupt the other team's rhythm.

3. It can be used as a tactical weapon to drive your opponents away from the net and allow your team to move in and take the offensive.

4. Used repeatedly, the lob can tire your opponents by forcing them to race back from the net or backpedal and stretch high to hit an overhead. This kind of overhead from deep in the court is not an easy shot to handle, and meanwhile — ideally — your team has rushed up to take over the net.

5. The offensive lob (hit low and hard with topspin) can counter an aggressive team that continually tries to take control of the net and always seems to be hugging that area. This lob is usually the most effective way to back them off.

6. A good lob can affect your opponent psychologically by giving him a chance to choke on the overhead return. A missed overhead probably triggers more frustration than any other mistake in tennis, and it tends to affect the next shot because the person is so angry about the one he just bungled. Of course, if your opponent hits the overhead properly, you lose the point, but this is expected, so I like the trade-off potential.

Having said all these great things about the lob, I'm careful about overrecommending it to most players, unless they are willing to practice, for a good lob is one of the toughest shots to pull off in doubles. And if you fail to execute it, you simply give your opponents an easy overhead smash — and increased confidence as the match progresses. People talk about lobs like they're nothing ("Oh, I'll just lob over

85 A–C Although deep, this player steps into his lob and confuses the net player, who has anticipated a drive. He suddenly swings upward for a beautifully disguised lob.

A

B

C

their heads"), but they rarely practice the shot under realistic conditions. Pancho Gonzalez, who took great pride in his explosive serve and net-attacking skills, would still go out and practice his lob, and he had one of the best lobs I've ever seen.

Avoiding the Shallow Lob

When lobbing, the most common and costly mistake you can make is to hit the ball shallow, since this usually forces you or your partner to run for cover as an opponent slams an overhead.

One reason that you might lob short is that you may be looking at your opponents out of the corner of your eye as you go to hit, a distraction that can cause you to slow up your swing unconsciously. Instead, think of a mental cue that will help block the other team from your peripheral vision, so you're free to concentrate on hitting through the ball and completing your stroke.

Another common mistake is to jab or poke at the ball instead of taking a full swing. When possible, hit forward through the ball with a low-to-high motion and complete your follow-through. This should keep you from slowing your swing before impact and jabbing at the ball. Also, when you run laterally or retreat backward for the ball and throw up a lob, you may not be compensating for the fact that your forces are going in the opposite direction, away from your intended target area. This can easily cause your lobs to come up short.

I also recommend that when you hit your first practice lob before a match, try to place it 5 to 10 feet too long, beyond the baseline. Trust me. For some reason, lobs rarely travel as far as anticipated, and your ball will very likely stay in bounds. If it does go long, don't worry; just hit your next one with exactly the same racket-head speed, but with a steeper forward-and-upward stroking motion, so that the extra length you had on the first lob will go into height and still give you the depth you seek.

If you're going to commit an error, strive to be too long with your lob rather than too short. You may get a lucky line call, and you won't hand your opponent a potential putaway overhead opportunity. Also, when you're near a baseline corner, try to lob on a diagonal to gain extra distance and thus more time to move into good position for your next shot. (Many people, when they practice lobs, watch the ball land 15 or 20 feet inside the baseline yet fail to realize this is an ineffective lob. They think, "It landed in, so that's good," but unless you're lobbing to within 10 feet of the baseline — and inside of 5 feet at the pro level — you're going to pay the price.)

Baseline Ground Strokes

From an evolutionary standpoint in doubles, you'll hit fewer traditional ground strokes from the baseline as you improve and play against better teams (unless, of course, you and your partner choose to play defensively by staying back on the baseline). In fact, let's go back 40 years to Talbert and Old's doubles book and their reminder (as true now as it was then) that few points are won from the backcourt position: "In doubles points are won from the net, not from the base line. So it stands to reason that the primary objective of back-court play is to get the devil out of the back court. A team should never willingly linger in the back court; if it is forced to retreat there it must maneuver to regain the net, and once an opening is gained it should set sail for the forecourt immediately."

Still, several common technique problems certainly tend to crop up on the baseline. Here are some reminders that should help when you need to drive the ball from here.

1. I've emphasized throughout the book how the pace of the game — especially at the advanced level — has increased dramatically in recent years, mainly because today's rackets generate so much power. That not only puts a premium on anticipation and reaction, but also dictates that strokes should be shorter and biomechanically more efficient in order for players to cope with the speed of the ball. Since modern rackets can generate nearly all the power you need on ground strokes, you can adopt a shorter, more compact — and more reliable — backswing and still hit as hard as ever. A more efficient swing will allow you to react more quickly and adjust to the rapid pace.

2. *Hit* the ball, don't baby it. This philosophy increases the risk of errors, but just trying to keep the ball in play from the

baseline against a team that has one player back and one player up is not enough. Driving the ball at either player, you must reduce the time they have to make decisions and reach the ball, while putting pressure on them to execute. When you start holding back, that's when all the problems really begin. (Of course, if your team is somehow caught on the baseline against a team with one player on the baseline and the other at the net, hit deep to that baseline player or bring him up with a short ball as you and your partner rush the net in tandem.)

3. Instead of backing up and hitting everything on the drop, learn to take the ball on the rise whenever possible. This doesn't necessarily send the ball back faster (our studies show), but it greatly reduces the time your opponents have to react to the shot and move to the ball. You don't beat them so much with the speed of this shot as with time reduction, and you also force different hitting rhythms on them. On the very same shot, an awful lot of people perform elegantly when they have time to wind up and blast the ball but hit quite poorly when they are rushed.

Hitting the ball on the rise is not as important in singles as in good doubles, especially when the other team is together near the net or trying to stay back and dink the ball all afternoon. Against dinkers, if you can take some of their high-bouncing, topspin shots on the rise (instead of backing up to hit everything on the downflight) and bring them in to the net with deliberate short balls, you will force them to hit approach shots and volleys, which they hate to do. Basically, you make life uncomfortable for them and this may help undermine their play.

Technically, most people have trouble taking the ball on the rise because their backswing is too long and they get caught late. If you can learn to keep the racket on the front side of your body as you take your backswing and move into the shot, taking balls on the rise becomes much easier. Also, the earlier you can catch the ball on the rise, the higher you can hit the ball over the net, because whoever's playing the net on the other team gets less time to react and make a move to cut the ball off.

4. Keep your head still through impact to (1) minimize the times you hit into the net, (2) keep from unconsciously slowing up on your swing, and (3) help yourself consistently hit the "sweet spot" on your strings. High-speed photography shows that when a player looks around just before impact, the racket also moves on a horizontal plane, causing him to net a lot of shots or contact the ball near the edge of the frame.

Staying "over" the ball (when the ball is arriving at about waist level or lower) is critical when you're returning the serve against a good net rusher, because you're shooting down a narrow alley — away from the netman — toward a small target area about 10 feet wide, near the service line. Many players tend to think that the wider court in doubles provides a bigger area to accommodate their ground strokes, but in reality they have only 18 feet in width against each opponent, compared with 27 feet in singles. This is why you must keep your head still and your eyes focused on the ball in order to help ensure solid, consistent contact.

When I point out this problem at my tennis college, people laugh and I see them

A

B

86 A–B In practice, player 2 is working on driving the ball between his opponents at the net, aiming for the plastic target (A). When his opponents are deep, he practices hitting the ball high over the net so that it lands deep and keeps them pinned on the baseline (B).

87 If you pull up too early to see where your shot is going to travel, the result will be a lot of balls hit off the edge of your strings.

A B C D

88 A–D The hitter sees an opportunity to get to the net. He chooses to hit the ball with a slight underspin to keep the ball low into his opponent's court (even though flat, hard drives actually stay lower than underspin if hit on the same trajectory). This will force his opponent to hit "up" and give him a higher volley. A fast start on the approach shot is also a major factor. The player hits forward with the racket face turned slightly upward (B) and is swinging in a small "banana-like" pattern (C). He finishes with his racket head high, which places his racket head in a perfect position for the next volley (D). It's important to run through the shot so that the racket head remains smooth. A stop-and-high motion forces the racket head down and places the hitter too far back from the net.

nudging their partners, because they recognize this as one of their problems, and it's no longer a mystery what causes it. And when we take photos of students hitting the ball, invariably their eyes are caught looking off into the distance at impact.

I'll agree, it's a big temptation to look up early to see where your shot is going, or to be distracted by your opponents' movements out of the corner of your eye when you fail to focus solely on the ball. So concentrate on a visual cue or a zone that will help keep you from abruptly pulling up off the shot just before impact. For example, try to keep your head still, and don't worry about tracking your shot until you hear the ball meet the racket. Or, focus on the impact point until you see your arm cross in front of your body. Then you can look up.

5. When your intended shot is clearly out of reach by the net player, and the other opponent is deep, visualize a target window about six feet above the net rather than a target area on the court, which can be seen only through the net. This should encourage you to hit with a safety margin over the net, while respecting physiological research, which shows that we tend to hit where our eyes are looking — so keep them off the net tape.

In intermediate tennis, you can consistently hit the ball high over the net from the baseline rather than gamble with net skimmers, because a lot of players at this level fail to poach, either on the serve or once the point is under way. Also, when you hit the ball low over the net, most opponents will simply run up and take it on the bounce, putting you on the defensive. But as you advance in doubles, your ground strokes must travel lower over the net in order to put pressure on a poacher, the server coming to the net, or two players at the net.

Still, if you can take a crosscourt ball and hit it down the line with topspin about five feet above the net, your opponent at the net must hit a high backhand volley — certainly a more difficult shot to handle than a forehand volley at about chest level. Just ask yourself: When you're hitting a high backhand volley at above head level, do you feel that this is a cinch putaway? I've known pros who lack that kind of confidence in this shot.

I've talked here about how the various individual shots provide the overall framework for a doubles team. In chapter 9 I'll illustrate some of the ways you can strengthen your team's interior "muscles" through specific practice drills.

CHAPTER 8

You, Psychology, and Your Partner

IS your team caught in the dilemma in which you and your partner have a great attitude on the court and everybody loves you around the club, but you keep losing in the first round? You could do with fewer laughs and more victories, right?

Quite likely, you've decided that your team's major hurdle is basically psychological. You want to know, for example, "What can we do to keep from choking?" Or perhaps you're wondering what clever ploys the two of you could be using against unsuspecting opponents. You may have even read my book *Mental Tennis,* searching for clues.

Well, we need to keep tennis psychology in perspective. Although I'm a licensed psychologist, when it comes to playing better tennis, I have always placed my emphasis on strokes over psychology, execution over mind games. I continue to feel strongly that everybody needs more than a great mental attitude to improve their play, in singles and doubles alike, and that stroke production is what underlines a winner. Positive thinking and strong psyches can indeed help give a team the occasional edge against equally talented opponents, but, ultimately, this team also needs the basic shots and close teamwork skills to win important matches, week in and week out.

For example, I feel that positive thinking is meaningful only when it's based on a person's stroking ability. If you're working on the tools you need to get the job done and paying your dues in practice, you'll be amazed at what some good strokes can do for your attitude. You may be feeling lousy when the match begins, but if you know you can crack off a crosscourt winner against the server as he rushes the net, you'll move to the ball thinking, "This return is a piece of cake." Conversely, if you have a crummy forehand and a crummy backhand, the most positive attitude in the world can't bail you out against slightly better players; it will just make it easier for you to lose with a smile on your face.

At virtually every level of play, winners rely on stroke production, while losers grasp at psychological games. A lethal volley is one of the best mental weapons I know. So the key question is this: Do you have the necessary weapons? If you're honest with yourself, this should lead you to work primarily on your strokes. I've found that usually people have psychological problems in tennis because, consciously or subconsciously, they know they don't have good strokes to support their aspirations, and their weak strokes help undermine their psychology and promote choking.

Of course, as you go to work on your strokes, the mental side of doubles is certainly still critical, and obviously more complicated than in singles, where you have a single opponent, since you must cope with two opponents and their particular — and peculiar — behavior, plus your partner's personality. Fortunately, there are immediate, practical mental strategies that can help you deal with various individual challenges, from how to channel your nerves when playing under tournament pressure to coping with various partnership conflicts.

Methods to Minimize Choking

When you and your partner find yourselves in a particularly competitive and challenging situation — a match against the league's best team, perhaps, or the semifinals of a tournament — are you sometimes so nervous that you have trouble playing up to your ability? Does your team play well in a big match until you get close to winning but then frequently fall apart? Do the two of you have difficulty handling the bizarre but seemingly calculated shenanigans of various opposing teams?

Take heart. These are typical problems in doubles everywhere that can be overcome with some advance thinking and good common sense out on the court. In fact, being nervous before a big match and having that "butterflies in the stomach" feeling is natural and can provide an advantage if you're aware of the effects on your body and psyche. And once the match is under way, a certain level of nervousness is critical to help most people stay alert and focused.

Here are some approaches to keep in mind, both as an individual player and in tandem with your partner.

1. No doubt about it, fears of losing or just "looking bad" can make a player so nervous that his or her game suffers. These psychological aspects are accentuated in doubles because there's a partner looking on as you hit — as well as two opponents — and this complicates whatever individual pressure you might feel or impose upon yourself in singles. You must deal with your perceptions of your partner's expectations and the perceived judgment and scrutiny by two opponents.

If you're continually worried about what your partner is thinking as he watches you play and you're thinking, "Jeez, I don't want to let him down," you're taking on unnecessary, self-inflicted pressure. Quite

A

B

C

89 A–C Here's another view of the approach shot, this time by a player hitting a two-hander but aggressively moving forward into the ball and continuing to the net without pausing. Notice how he keeps his eyes focused on the ball and his racket up on the follow-through.

likely, it could be stemming from your childhood experiences in sports if you harbored strong feelings about not wanting to let your parents or your teammates down.

2. If you're playing to *win,* establish realistic goals for your team, one week to the next. Unhappy players are those who set unattainable goals.

3. Have an objective game plan already worked out when you arrive for the match, but with an understanding that you've also practiced the strokes that support this game plan, so that the probability of performing better is greater. Preparation like this tends to ease individual anxiety, which should help you and your partner play up to your abilities.

4. Another way to boost confidence and help control nerves going into a match is to take a realistic approach to your stroking problems by actually working on them between matches — not simply when you are warming up.

5. Richard Schmidt, a motor-learning expert at UCLA, reminds us: "Take care of

A

B

90 A–C When forced to hit a low volley or a half-volley against an attacking team, your goal is to keep the ball away from the net man. If your half-volley goes to the player on the right (A), he now has a putaway volley opportunity, but continue moving forward to put visual pressure on him as he hits (B). Ideally, you want to angle the ball crosscourt and low so that your opponent must bend for a half-volley of his own (C), allowing you and your partner to move confidently forward, knowing he must lift the ball.

C

stroking details when you practice, but just hit the ball when you play, keeping your mind off the isolated parts." Research shows that when you simply go out and *hit* the ball during a match, you're closer to the desired stroke than when you try to concentrate on specific details.

6. Remind yourself that the best you can do is to make a strong effort in every department and have some fun while you're doing it. Measure the penalty you feel you have to pay for losing — such as disappointing your loved ones at home or suffering embarrassment in front of fellow club members — against the fun you receive from winning. Sometimes society's penalties are too great. If you're thinking, "I'm playing with my boss, and if we lose, I

could jeopardize my job," then you really should think about changing your job.

7. Don't let yourself be intimidated by an opponent's clothes or equipment.

8. People hardly ever play the way they warm up, so don't let yourself be easily filled with boundless optimism or unbridled gloom.

9. Laugh off the attempted "psych" jobs. A player who attempts to psych out his opponents is usually a person who lacks all the weapons he needs to beat them straight. Besides, I'm not a believer that someone actually psychs you out; instead, you allow this person to manipulate you.

10. You may not give much thought to concentration until you realize you're playing poorly or carelessly, at which point you may begin banging your racket against your body while admonishing yourself, "Concentrate, dummy, concentrate!" Concentrating on concentration is actually distracting, so, instead, kill the internal dialogue and just hit the ball. There's no time in doubles to say, "Concentrate, dummy!" because the ball will be past you while you're talking.

(The key point about concentration is to focus only on those things that will help you execute a good shot. Anything else is a contaminant. Go through a self-evaluation, asking yourself, "When I do this, is it meaningful? Does it help me get to the ball faster? Does it help keep my mind on the game?" After going through a little checklist, dump those things that fail to contribute.)

11. Minimize the number of things you think about as you play. Some players become so overwhelmed with details about stroke production and tactics that it detracts from their play — and their enjoyment. Instead of worrying about sophisticated tactics, know what your role is on-court — at all four positions — and stick to the basics I've stressed in this book. That is, serve to the side (backhand or forehand) that produces the highest and longest return from your opponent; move into the net at every opportunity; keep your returns low (against a net-rushing server) and away from the net person; go for the angles; hit down the middle when your opponents are at the net, but don't overlook the sidelines; and keep on the move and be thinking, "The next shot's coming to me."

12. If you happen to be a good singles player who has trouble playing well in doubles, it could be that you're "thinking" too much out on the court and it's leaving you confused and indecisive. The next time you play doubles, resolve ahead of time that instead of doing so much evaluating on the court, you're going to start programming yourself to focus only on the key fundamentals. For example, aim your return of serve at a specific target area, away from the net person; lob when you're in trouble and your opponents are at the net; keep the ball low and down the middle as much as possible; and move in tandem with your partner, always trying to gain control of the net.

13. As you play, learn to rule out external stimuli and extraneous thoughts, which can inhibit your swing and keep you from executing your best stroke. Instead of thinking about your opponents, on the other side of the net, as the ball comes toward you, or being distracted by their movement, decide on your shot and reduce mental "clutter" so that you're free to make the hit.

After the match, try to record notes

A

B

91 A–B Always be striving to move forward with your partner so that you can volley as many balls as possible before they fall too low. Also keep moving forward as a team as you volley.

about what kind of distractions there were and at what point they surfaced. After doing this for several matches you may realize, for instance, that you have more extraneous thoughts once the score reaches deuce than early in the point, and this may help you solve the riddle as to why your play seems to suffer on the big points.

14. Don't waste your energy, concentration, and goodwill by getting mad. Nobody enjoys hearing or seeing expressions of anger, such as swearing or racket tossing — except in tournament play, when angry players make opponents happy.

15. Try to avoid getting discouraged by your opponent's unbelievable saves. The video highlight plays tend to even out in most matches.

16. Focus on the ball and treat each shot with respect.

92 Both players should stay focused on the ball and be ready to move.

17. When you get into tight situations — like deuce, with the set tied at 5-all — don't let pressure dictate your shot selection. Hit the shot that should be hit under the circumstances, whatever the score, and avoid thinking, "I just want to play it safe and get out of this point alive." Instead of opting for a safe but imprudent shot just to keep the ball in play, always go for the shot you know you should take, whether you're winning or losing, and you'll feel good about yourself, while also having more success at the game. The score is going to be tied 5-all the rest of your life; this isn't the only 5-all shot in America today, so hit the ball and have some fun.

Communicating with Your Partner During a Match

Talking about why her partnership with Natasha Zvereva was so successful (six Grand Slam titles at that point) and what she felt she brought to the team, Gigi Fernandez told Jerry Crowe of the *Los Angeles Times*,

> It's a lot of technical things [Zvereva's versatile serve, Fernandez's solid volleys and a strong serve] but I think more important than anything is my personality. I communicate well and I'm easy to get along with on the court and I'm very supportive of my partners. And I think in

a doubles partnership, that's the main thing, because, at this level, everybody has the strokes. Most people can develop a good doubles game. It's just a matter of being able to find somebody that you can get along with and communicate with when things aren't going so well.

Actively and openly communicating with your partner, through good times and bad on the court, is a key to good doubles — and your enjoyment of the game. Rather than allowing yourselves to play quietly together, in set patterns, try to emphasize communication with each other throughout the match and having flexibility in your tactics.

For instance, when your team is playing well but your own game is particularly hot and you think you can win key points by stretching out a bit more (e.g., poaching near the net after the point is under way), you shouldn't even have to ask your partner, "Let me be a little more aggressive here because I'm really hitting well today." You should be poaching more and trying for more shots — and your partner should automatically sense that it's working, and not feel defensive. Meanwhile, the philosophy should also work the other way, when you say to your partner, "Hey, keep it going, way to hit" when he's playing great and is more aggressive about taking shots that normally would belong to you. He should never feel that he has to ask you for the "freedom" to do this. That's the kind of rapport, the instincts, you should develop and nurture.

Another situation that can arise on a particular day is a partner who feels lousy and can't cover the court as well as usual, who tells you, "Look, I can barely move — I'm really dragging today — so you have to do the best you can to cover for me; you have to take everything you can reach and cover my lobs." You should be prepared to play one against two like this, because we can all relate to having a partner start to come unglued in the second set on a hot day, or after a hot evening. It is critical that both of you be free to adjust like this.

Also, what about those matches in which nothing is going right for your team? Can you find ways to turn the match into something fun, or at least into a learning experience, where you experiment with a different strategy just to see what happens?

Taming the Court Hog

Wherever I travel, battle-scarred women from mixed doubles invariably want to know, "What should I do about a partner who tries to hog all the shots? He thinks he's better than he actually is, so he tries to play the whole court, and that spoils the fun for me. This usually happens in club and social events and it sometimes can get pretty irritating, especially when he's really no better than I am. How can I assert myself and tactfully deal with this without causing a scene?"

If you want your partner to be less of a court hog — assuming that he's not moving in for legitimate shots as the player closest to the net — start by expressing your dissatisfaction. Tell him, "Look, it's not much fun for me when you try to take all the shots. I'm not really playing doubles here, I'm watching you play singles, so we have to talk this out." More often than not, just revealing how you feel will help resolve the problem, unless the guy's an incorrigible chauvinist, in which case you have little choice but to dissolve the team. If it's a little more difficult than that — he's your husband, for example — you need to gather some objective statistics that can help support your complaints.

One approach is to have a friend chart one of your team's matches, recording who made what errors, and then have these results analyzed by a computer firm such as CompuTennis. Then the data are quantifiable, and you can show your partner: "Look, you hit eighty-two volleys, and only twenty-four landed in the court; I hit only sixteen, but twelve went for putaways."

"Intent" is also a key issue here. Does your partner seem to take your legitimate shot arbitrarily, as though stealing something from you, or does he make the play because he knows he should take this shot in order to help your team win the point? You need to distinguish between his right (and obligation) to volley your shot if he's indeed closer to the net and his evident intention to go after every shot he can reach and not let you have an opportunity to play doubles the way it ought to be played. If you truly suspect his intent is to go after every shot regardless of whose it legitimately is, and you talk to him about it and he doesn't change, then the problems are deeper than you can resolve in doubles and it's time to think about canceling the partnership.

Partnership Conflicts

Competitively, the biggest mistake a doubles team can make is to think that no major psychological or emotional problems will erupt or develop between them as they play together. Rather, you and your partner should anticipate these potential eventualities and have the groundwork laid for resolving the little incompatibilities that can spoil the fun and tear apart a partnership based on tennis.

What counts the most, I think, is to agree upon a "laugh and win" theme with your partner. This means going out and giving your best effort to win, but with the intent of having some fun and keeping everything positive while supporting each other in the spirit of "We win together and we lose together." When the two of you embrace this philosophy, the precarious psychological moments can be more easily handled and, indeed, will arise less often. You'll realize that suppressing anger and frustration and resentment toward a partner, or going at each other's throat when things aren't going well, is unrewarding and ultimately destructive. Instead, the "laugh and win" philosophy, discussed before you've actually played a match together, should provide a groundwork for averting — or at least minimizing — the various disputes that can arise in any doubles relationship.

For example, when terrible things are happening to a good player — *you* — on a day when you clearly are making most of the errors, you must somehow remain confident and not succumb to frustration, since a lot more shots are going to be coming your way as the other team attacks the weak link. Here's where you need not only internal fortitude and a better volley but also a partner's open support. You need a partner who starts taking more balls down the middle and assures you, "Don't worry, just keep playing hard; you'll get back on your game." You want a partner who is strong enough to respond to your problem in a healthy way, not someone who snipes at you with barbs such as "God, can't you get one service return back?" or "That's about five overheads you've missed. I've got to start taking all of them."

Preserving the desired partnership rapport also assumes that you have equal toleration for your partner's mistakes. This means thinking to yourself, "Hey, he missed it, but he was aggressive and he got to the ball; it was his shot to take. That's the way it goes." And meanwhile, you do your best to carry the load, without playing the martyr's role.

This is all part of establishing an understanding, a process, whereby both of you know that one partner is going to play crummy sometimes and the other person is going to try to rise to the occasion to compensate, and vice versa. It's like a marriage, in that when things are going right for both people, it's great, but this doesn't always happen. And so, as a tennis partnership, you're really preparing for the good times and the lousy times as a team.

Depersonalizing the Relationship

As I've pointed out, virtually every great doubles team will have to deal with some kind of emotional blowup between partners, and you should anticipate this happening on your own team. The key question becomes, when a blowup does occur, Can you take an emotional hurt and go forward? If you find that your emotions are too easily bruised in doubles, then you really should stick to singles.

At a Virginia Slims tournament at La Costa in 1993, I saw an interesting example of how just one incident can suddenly trigger unexpected, pent-up emotions — and how important it is to explore the underlying problem quickly, on behalf of the partnership.

The number-one team in the world, Gigi Fernandez and Natasha Zvereva, was playing, and an overhead opportunity arose between them, down the center. Fernandez was ready for the shot and said, "I've got it," but Zvereva also said, "I've got it," and even though she was backing up and had a less desirable hitting position, she took the shot and hit a weak overhead that the other team returned for a winner. Fernandez was so disgusted that even though the winning shot came close to her, she simply stood there and swiped it into the net. Her body language clearly said frustration and anger, and she "tanked" another shot before cooling down. This apparently was the first time she had publicly lost her patience and displayed emotion of this nature. But Zvereva's interference had suddenly brought to the surface other factors that could no longer be contained by Fernandez. Their coach, Julie Anthony, a clinical psychologist, later told me it was one of the first times she had seen a personalization of something like that between them.

Fortunately, and to her credit, Fernandez made an effort to resolve the problem immediately after the match. She and Zvereva evaluated what had happened, cleared the air, and went on to win the tournament — and many more championships after that.

This ability to depersonalize the relationship the best you can, and not become co-dependent, is crucial for holding a doubles team together. Otherwise, if you're not careful, you'll begin to take out personal frustrations on your partner, triggered by something he or she does on the tennis court but actually reflecting something else that's going on in your life that has nothing to do with this particular tennis match. So it's very important that your partner — the recipient of your behavior — learn to disassociate himself or herself from this behavior and avoid becoming co-dependent, thinking, "Yeah, I'm letting her down; I'm screwing the whole thing up." When a person is having a lousy day on the court, adding guilt to the frustration is almost a guarantee that he or she will play even worse as the match progresses. (Speaking as a psychological adviser here, if your not-so-subtle intent is indeed to add guilt, you have a more severe problem than your partner because your intent is to hurt.)

If your team has some ground rules established and good things aren't happening between the two of you, and you're getting mad about it, be aware that you may actually be responding to childhood emotions and experiences. When one of the ground rules that you set with your partner is being ignored right before your eyes, your anger may have nothing to do with your partner, but instead be about experiences you had as a child, such as parents and coaches who were upset with you when you didn't perform well or who pinned everything on winning or who gave you a sense that you were being accepted only if you played well. All of these things could now be surfacing on the tennis court, triggered by your partner's behavior, but actually stemming from somewhere in your childhood.

Again, what counts is for you and your partner to discuss these human factors early in the relationship so that you've aired the possibilities and there are no real personality surprises once you begin playing together and an important match is under way. There are enough surprises in the course of a normal match.

Go through some of the scenarios that could arise. For instance, you might say, "Look, there are going to be days when one of us is going to be making every mistake in the book. You know that and I know that. What's important is that it not become a personalized thing and for each of us to recognize this and admit, 'I'm having one of those statistical days. How do I compensate and let you try to bail us out?'" Similarly, if your partner admits that this is going to be a dreadful day before you even get on the court, he should be able to tell you so. Perhaps you both can agree that trying to focus on the match will be therapeutic.

Signs of a Troubled Partnership

I feel there should be two criteria involved when we play tennis: to try to win and to have fun. If you're losing and playing with the wrong partner, you're 0 for 2, which means the worst possible predicament in the sport. But if you can find a partner who helps makes it fun, this can literally compensate for one loss after another, which puts you closer to a win-win situation.

Here's where it's instructive to note how every so often, from the club level to the pro level, two players will join up and have an unbelievably great tournament the first time they ever play together. Obviously there are special dynamics at work, not only in terms of how their tennis games happen to mesh so well, but also in terms of the psychological factors they bring to the partnership. For example, they both seem to try hard to please their partner, to show how well they can play and what a nice personality they possess. They haven't settled into a "marriage" and started bickering about this or that, but instead begin each match with a clean slate, intent on trying their hardest, as individuals and as a team.

A strong tournament performance by rookie teammates proves to me, for one thing, that a good doubles team doesn't necessarily need to play together a long time in order to be successful. And it also reflects the spirit that every doubles team should try to retain after the honeymoon wears off.

Alas, personality and psychological conflicts do begin to emerge as teammates play together, so it's important to explore some of the signs that a tennis partnership is in trouble and perhaps ought to be abandoned — for the sake of your enjoyment. (In fairness to your partner, you should try to answer or address these questions from his or her perspective.)

1. Does your partner talk to you? You may prefer a strong, silent type, but to play best as a team, match in and match out, there should be constant communication between the two of you. Some of it will concern the previous point and your ongoing strategy, while some of it should be more personal — how each of you is feeling. A good doubles team will have their heads together after nearly every point, whispering, plotting the next point, giving each other support.

2. Does your partner appear to give her best effort throughout the match, even when her play is off or your team is getting crunched? Or does she tend to give up? Does she cover her own area and responsibilities, or do you suddenly find yourself crossing into her court, trying to chase down every ball? If so — and if this bothers you but you don't know how to bring the subject up — just be aware that this competitive incompatibility is going to fester and turn from irritation to tremendous frustration the longer you play together.

3. Psychologically, how well does your partner handle defeat? The two of you may have a lot of fun together when you're winning, but if he is miserable when you lose and so upset that he embarrasses you with his boorish on-court behavior, you should question whether it's worth playing together.

4. What about your teammate's response when you're in the midst of losing a match? Afterward, you might discuss a possible scenario from this perspective: "I know we were both down when we started losing today, but I thought one of our goals was to remain positive and try to support each other in that kind of situation. I felt I had to try to pick you up, and I made every effort, but it didn't seem to work — I couldn't tell what was going through your head. Have I read you right? Did you have the same feelings about me?" Try to elicit responses from your partner with an open approach like this, so that you can clarify potential misunderstandings early in the relationship.

5. How well does your partner share responsibility for the team's wins and losses? While he may be an excellent singles player, can he share the glory — as well as the blame? That's tough for a lot of players to do in doubles, particularly those with highly egocentric personalities.

6. Does your partner continue to support your play even on those days when the two of you are constantly going up to the net to retrieve most of your shots? A telltale sign of a troubled partnership is the growing realization that your partner is increasingly hostile and distancing when you keep making errors on key points, regardless whether she's playing well or not. You'll recognize the dissatisfaction, because few players can hide the body language: the barely concealed look of disgust when you dump yet another shot into the net; the silent treatment; the biting voice that has a "give me a break" tone; the reluctance even to move for the next ball; the head down as she ignores you, just looking at her feet; the rolling of her eyes; the walking away from you, instead of coming closer to offer support.

I've discovered over the years that few players have difficulty identifying a partner who is seething inside. It doesn't matter what the body signals were out on the court; when I sit down to interview a player after a match, the person will say, "Gee, my partner was really upset." The partner may have been trying hard not to reveal that frustration, yet it still surfaced.

If you sense anger in your partner about the way you're performing — even if it's unspoken — or if you have unresolved anger about your partner, you should bring it out into the open as something you really owe to each other. There are some tricky little issues that can sometimes be ironed out, but there are other things that say, "Hey, we're better off to be apart."

Another psychological aspect to consider here, as you perhaps try to resolve conflict with your partner, is the realization that no one can make you angry. Instead, you choose to feel anger. Even therapists who have never been on a tennis court will tell you that when you start reminding yourself, "I choose to get angry . . . I choose to be happy," you're placing blame in the right direction, and you can begin to look at yourself from a more realistic perspective. For example, you can ask yourself, "Why did I choose the anger? Why did I choose sadness?" If you can learn to think this way in doubles as you assess the partnership, the result should be a more realistic and much healthier relationship.

7. Do you have the sense that you're letting your partner down every time you make a mistake? Be honest with yourself here. If the feelings of playing doubles and letting somebody down are just too severe, whether it be a friend or a family member, I would recommend getting out of the partnership and avoiding a serious commitment to doubles until you find somebody you are very comfortable with — as a tennis player and as a person.

To enjoy doubles, you must let go of the little hurts during a match and, as I suggested earlier, not take them personally. If you're really thinking about the best interests of your partner as you play, you almost always get the best interest for yourself back. If you don't get this treatment back — and you are indeed making this effort — it's time to end the partnership. Always remember: You have a right to be happy playing doubles.

Ending the Partnership

When starting out with any doubles partner, remind yourself that as kind-hearted as you might be, you don't "owe" that person a second match. If your initial pairing together proves a little disappointing, yet still seems to have promise, you may want to have a discussion and then go forward and try another match or two. But if you realize you've misjudged the person — as a player, a competitor, a potential companion, or whatever — and the relationship is unlikely going to prove successful, just be as honest and direct as you can.

Of course, broaching the fact that one's team should break up is certainly not easy for most people, which may help explain why some partnerships endure 20 or 30 years for otherwise unfathomed reasons. Quite understandably, most people simply don't have the skills or the nerve to be honest with a tennis partner and say, "I'm not comfortable any longer when we play — somehow we're not meshing, and I think we need new partners." This is an uncomfortable admission (and a perceived accusation) at best, but it's so much better to be honest and up front with your partner that it's just not working out, instead of harboring your unhappiness and resentment. Be honest with your feelings instead of hiding them.

Another inhibition may be that you're looking for a graceful way to end the relationship. But how? This is why I emphasize having prior discussions and setting some ground rules with your intended long-term partner before you ever play together. When you have an understanding between yourselves about ending the partnership, then either of you can more easily bring up the subject and neither will feel trapped.

Remember, even if the two of you are married to each other, this is not a marriage on the tennis court; it's a partnership that should increase the pleasure you gain from the game and from being with each other. When that relationship produces more aggravation than pleasure, it's time to find another tennis partner. Now, of course, I realize it's not always that easy, especially if your partner is a close friend or a business associate or a loved one. You may even be thinking, "Well, I can't do that so easily, Vic. You see, it's my wife." If it is your spouse, this can be a hard admission to make, but love should make no difference. Your fun in life is really more important than continuing to play with a person who is spoiling your fun, spoiling the experience. A decision now, in fact, could help save your marriage.

Another reason you may have difficulty is that you're embarrassed at having to tell your partner that you no longer want to play with him and afraid you will hurt his feelings. This indeed may be true, but I've often found that when the other person also knows that it's not the right relationship, he or she is equally relieved to have it end. If a person can hate you for being honest with him, he has his own problems to work out, and it's not your problem or your responsibility to feel guilty at what has happened. We tend not to want to tell people a relationship is over because we're afraid to hurt them. More often, however, the issue is about hurting ourselves. And how do you know it's actually going to hurt them to learn that you no longer want to play doubles with them? This may, in fact, come as a relief to them.

One way to give yourself a reasonably

objective sense of whether your partnership should continue or not is to draw up a list of questions, such as "Do I really look forward to playing doubles with this person? What do I like about it? What don't I like about it?" If you realize that you are actually unenthusiastic about playing a match tomorrow with this person, and if you have other similar feelings, this is something that should be worked out with your partner.

What counts is having fun — win or lose — and if you sense this isn't happening with your partner, or is not going to happen, it's important to be honest and up front about the situation. Certainly, when teams split up, it's not the end of the world. There are many fun times to be had with other partners, and there's often a sense of new energy. When Martina Navratilova and Pam Shriver broke up after winning numerous Grand Slam events, Pam was devastated, but she came back with a new partner the following year and won the U.S. doubles title. And South African Frew McMillan won one major event after another (especially mixed doubles) with one partner after another.

If you're not having fun playing doubles, finding a new partner may provide the solution. When you think about the situation, it could be that you have to "chill out" a little bit and look more for the fun that's inherent in the game — or simply find a person who's just as competitive as you are.

CHAPTER 9

Practice Drills to Make You "Famous by Friday"

IF your team's success has plateaued and you're seeking a higher level, improved court coverage and some new tactics adopted from this book will help out. More important, however, my bet is that you and your partner need to pay greater attention to individual stroke production. When you improve your various shots, everything else, starting with strategy, will fall more effectively into place.

Doubles practice is the most underrated, overlooked part of the game, at every level. I mean, how often do you hear a couple of players say, "We're going out to practice our doubles?" There's a tendency to think that improvement will come simply by playing a lot of singles and doubles matches. In reality, though, the serve, service return, and volley should all be practiced with doubles in mind. So should specific doubles moves, alone and with your partner. Take time to practice the elements I emphasize in this chapter and your team will, in short order, make a quantum leap past teams that are beating you now but failing to practice. Teams that fail to improve their weaknesses in practice must live with the same weaknesses match after match.

When you try the drills in this chapter and throughout the book, note that they are as realistic as possible. This reflects my personal preference as a coach and what I've learned from motor-learning research, which shows that if your practice drills are unrelated to what actually happens in a match, they are almost worthless as a learning device. Drills should relate to the actual playing demands out on the court. This means, quite simply, that as you work on your serve, try to have your partner practice his return; as you concentrate on placing your serve, he can aim for crosscourt targets and lob returns, also at targets.

In this chapter, I'll focus on how to improve some of the key individual shots and movements demanded in good doubles. Even if you work on only three strokes — (1) a more dependable serve (along with developing a slice), (2) a more aggressive but well-aimed service return, and (3) a sharper volley — your improvement will give your team an enormous lift, since these are the most important strokes in doubles. I also want to emphasize movement and anticipation drills that will help you cover the court and move to the ball more effectively, which in turn will help position you to hit the ball properly more often.

The Serve

I've long been intrigued by the fact that the serve is the only stroke in tennis over which we have complete control, yet it is the one that breaks down most often. Fortunately, you can get out on an empty court by yourself with a basket of balls and work on improving your serve without having to rely on a practice partner.

My major focus here will be the slice serve (reflecting my earlier emphasis on this particular stroke in chap. 7), mastering a toss that travels out in front of the body, and quick footwork as you fall in and advance toward the net.

Developing a Slice Serve

Hitting a slice requires the same technique used for flat and topspin serves, and should indeed present the same "look" to your opponent, so that you camouflage your intentions to force him wide off the deuce court. The only stroking difference should be where you contact the ball as your racket comes across and imparts sidespin rotation.

A Better Toss to Minimize Choking

In chapter 7, I stressed the importance of having a toss that is comfortably out in front of the body and to the right, so that you are already on the way to the net as you contact the ball. The common mistake here is a straight-up toss, which forces the player to contact the ball above his head instead of comfortably out ahead of the body.

By tossing the ball on a forward-moving arc, you can hit the ball hard with a snapping forearm action as your body unwinds into the shot and the racket travels fast. This helps ensure a smooth, rhythmical motion that saves the hitting shoulder, and at contact you'll already be on your way to the net with forward momentum. (People wonder why a singles player like Andre Agassi, as hard as he serves, can't go to the net successfully against players with strong service returns. We studied Agassi on high-speed film, and the answer was clear: Andre jumps off the ground so high when he serves that instead of moving forward as he contacts the ball, he has to wait for gravity to bring him down, and thus when the ball crosses the net, his left foot is just landing. This means he's too far back to attack the net with any real success. Of course, he has still managed to win Wimbledon and the U.S. Open, but think of the lost potential.)

Tossing the ball directly above your

A

B

93 A–C The server is working on coiling and uncoiling his body for more power. He makes certain his toss is well in front of the service line (A), and he pushes off with his left foot for a good start (B). Notice, though, we caught him in a foot fault. He then begins his first step toward the net after his initial service step (C).

C

head constricts the swing and forces you to recruit muscles earlier than is natural in order to contact the ball. By doing so, you also lose the fourth link in a desired sequence by the body — and thus potential power.

There's another crucial reason why I advocate grooving a toss that arcs well out in front of the body. We know from electromyography studies that when people are having trouble with their serve and begin to choke, they tend to draw back, since "back" — closer to the body — means safety. I know, this may sound Freudian here, but out on the tennis court, a server's fears and frustrations can bring the ball

94 A–E Practicing his serve, this player brings his throwing arm back to guarantee a desired body turn, while keeping the racket head down (A–B). The ball is tossed on the right side, which will allow him to move further forward on the hit while protecting his options to hit a slice or flat serve (C). His elbow begins to move forward before going upward to meet the ball (D). This allows the kinetic chain to stay intact. Going up, the racket head is on edge, which preserves the ability to pronate the forearm for more speed (E).

toss back, which forces him to recruit muscles earlier than desired, leading to an awkward feeling and a weak serve. This phenomenon is especially evident on second serves and at tight moments in a match when a person is struggling with his first serve.

Knowing this, you should try to avoid trouble by exaggerating your toss, throwing it seemingly too far in front, so that you counteract the psychology at work. In fact, when it comes to executing under pressure, "safety" is actually out away from the body, not back close.

While working on your serve, pay attention to the follow-up footwork that

A

B

95 A–B The server practices his footwork to the net. His back foot comes across the line first (A) as he moves forward, and when he takes his check step, he's flying (B). I don't recommend getting airborne like this because a player can't break in any direction until he lands.

can help make you a feared volleyer in singles and doubles alike. The goal here is to get as close to the net as possible to volley or half-volley your opponent's return, and it starts with your fall-in step, a second step, and a third, at which point you can "read" your opponent's return and move to your shot. In order to gain encouragement here, measure how far you now advance behind your serve by the time your opponent makes contact. Then measure how far you get after practicing your toss (further out in front of your body) and quicker footwork. You'll normally hit a ball from a higher position when you get further in, thus improving your chances of winning the point. Same shot, same technique, but against a ball closer to the net. Also, you won't have to contend with nearly as many returns that land at your feet.

The Service Return

This shot deserves particular attention in doubles, because statistically it's quite likely the only ball you will hit in the rally. Even in intermediate tennis, the ball tends to cross the net a maximum of five times. People tend to think that the service return is only the beginning of a long sequence, when basically it is just about the end.

Another reason to focus on the service return in practice is that it must be hit crosscourt and short, against one serve after another, when the server rushes the net. There's much more freedom to aim the ball in singles, even when the server moves in behind his serve. But against a net-rushing server in doubles, as we know, the ongoing challenge is to return the ball safely away from the net player, at or near the server's feet, so that he must bend down and lift his shot, allowing your team to move in for a good volley opportunity. (Many club players, of course, never come to the net behind their serve; in this case, they should try to hit higher and deeper returns away from the net player to gain more time to get to the net.)

At a practice session, place on-court targets near the service line and then have somebody hit you a succession of serves from both sides while you concentrate on hitting forehands and backhands to where an opponent would likely be advancing to the net behind his serve. Practice these returns over and over again as you determine the speed and the upward angle at which you should contact the ball in order to hit your intended targets.

Meanwhile, practice staying over the ball as you hit. This habit is especially critical on service returns, where it's easier to be distracted by having an opponent already up at the net as you swing and to feel more constrained as you hit than it is in singles. The service return is also more predictable in doubles than in singles because you know you should be aiming for the net rusher. So keep your head down, hit out, and don't look up until you've made contact. Practice this shot until it becomes as automatic and programmed as possible; then it doesn't matter who's at the net or who's coming to the net — you know the shot you want to hit.

In a match, when the net person likes to poach, a crosscourt return is still your best shot, forcing that person to make the play. Just avoid looking up early, since impatience can cause you to hit the ball erratically and with greater chance of error.

Also practice using spin to your advantage on the return. Hitting with a low-to-

A

B

96 A–B Doubles is a game of serve and service return. If there are only two players available, one partner can work on his or her serve and the other can work on service returns. Here, the receiver has laid out his predetermined service-return target.

high motion to impart topspin off the forehand side produces a shot that can be hit hard but safely over the net before it dips sharply down. On the backhand side, when you slice the ball low, it stays low after hitting the court, not because of the spin but because of the trajectory that it travels. You can practice these shots by setting up appropriate target areas on the court and then hitting off a ball machine or a hitting partner.

When you practice the service return, concentrate on getting a fast first step on a diagonal toward the net and reaching the ball quickly, so that you can step forward as you hit and make solid contact. Edging backward when the serve comes usually causes the body to be leaning back and the racket face to be tilted back as it comes into the impact zone, resulting in a high, ineffective return.

If you're always late against a fast serve, here's a drill to improve your anticipation skills and your ability to break earlier toward the ball. Have your partner or a friend hit 20 or 30 serves as you practice guessing where the ball is going to travel as soon as you see it come off the racket. After you've studied a server's motion and ball toss, you'll find that your original decisions are usually the most appropriate.

Also, play a singles match against a strong server and try to guess the serve's direction and just go for it, even if you're dead wrong. Trust your initial instincts and practice breaking in one direction or the other, and you'll be quite surprised at how often your original judgments are correct. But don't forget to move *forward* into the ball as you guess to which side it's coming.

This means working on your footwork. Wait for the serve in a high but comfortable body position, so that your first move can be toward the ball, not upward from a crouching position. Then make sure you're getting up on the balls of your feet as the server makes his toss. This prestretches your muscles, which facilitates moving quickly with short, rapid steps to the left or right. Make certain your weight is leaning slightly forward as you rise.

In doubles, especially, with an opposing player poised at the net waiting to crunch your weak return, you can't afford to sit back and raise the ball. You must drive it, and this means reaching every serve as quickly as possible in order to contact the ball out in front of your body. This is especially true on the backhand side (for one-handed backhand hitters), which is less forgiving than the forehand when a person wants to return the ball aggressively. On the forehand side, the shoulder housing the racket arm is away from the net, allowing slightly more hitting time. On the backhand, the hitting shoulder is on the front side of the body, and lateness will force you into a defensive style of play in which you must block the return or try to hit with underspin, when the goal is to play offensively.

If you want to hit a better service return against the fast serve, remember this: The better you get, the shorter your swing will be. Rotate your shoulders with a quick initial movement, taking the racket back to the top of the "C," so that you only have to let it drop as you swing into the ball. The time you now have available can be spent positioning for placement of your return. Watch how fast Pete Sampras gets his racket back, and the same with Steffi Graf — a rapid backswing, with the racket high and ready to fall.

The Volley

Earlier (page 63), I showed what it means to hit a good low volley by bending low and "playing" with a low-to-high shoulder action instead of relying on the forearm. In practice and as you play, constantly try to ingrain the idea that you're aiming for target windows above the net rather than target areas on the court when you volley. This will reinforce the importance of swinging toward the intended target above the net, in order to keep the ball out of the net.

Notice how the volleyer in photos 97 A–B has a friend hold a racket up at the net as he aims for different heights on the racket from various positions on the court. He concentrates on punching the ball through these "windows," safely above the net, in order to hit his on-court targets. Be warned that when people test their volleys with the window concept, they are almost always stunned that the window they think they must hit is actually far too low.

Also, I would reiterate: As you practice, realize just how hard you can actually volley a four-foot-high ball from the service line and keep it in play. This concept is important because just getting the ball back on the volley won't win many points in doubles; you must put your opponents on the defensive and capitalize on openings in their defense with sharply hit balls.

One excellent way to help improve your high backhand volley is to strengthen the extensor muscles in your hitting arm, so that you can return the ball deep or sharply angled. If you lack a strong arm (as well as an aggressive attitude), you'll tend to hit the ball short and give your opponents an easy putaway shot. But if you can keep the

A

B

97 A–B During a practice session, the player in the foreground practices his deep volley by aiming at his partner's racket above the net.

head of your racket up and "muscle" that ball, your opponents are in trouble.

The Lob

As tough as it is to hit a high, deep lob under pressure in doubles, I want to repeat how crucial this shot can be to your team's overall success. I think one important reason why most players fail to practice the lob is that, psychologically, the lobber doesn't realize the strength of the shot, regardless whether the point is won or lost. Many top players who are slightly out of shape can be worn out chasing down lobs, and the lob can enable a team to take over control of the net. Yet in intermediate tennis, especially, most players perceive the lob as an "all or nothing" shot, and they don't like that feeling, so they avoid it.

The most important thing about practicing lobs is to try to do so under realistic conditions, hitting them in situations and from locations you'll encounter in doubles. For example, instead of hitting lobs from a stationary position at the center of the court behind the baseline (which is not even realistic in singles), do the following:

- Have a practice partner hit balls that force you to lob on the move as you run along the baseline and off the court.

- When you're driven wide off the court, try hitting a deep crosscourt lob.

- Strive to hit target areas four to six feet inside the baseline, learning how high you must hit the ball by observing where the ball lands relative to

A

B

98 A–B When practicing your service return, try to find an opponent who can hit a "kick" (American twist) serve so that you can become familiar at detection and execution. That big back arch (A) is a good clue that a big spin serve is coming and it could likely kick to your left (B).

99 Players at my tennis college practice lobbing the ball deep, up to 10 feet *beyond* the baseline, so that they become familiar with that sensation. Then they learn how much they have to adjust the upward angle of their swing in order to bring the ball down *inside* the baseline.

the speed and upward angle of your swing.

- Retreat from the net to chase down a lob over your head, then throw up a lob of your own, as deep as you can, remembering to compensate for the fact that your momentum is going away from your intended target area.

The Overhead

Even though the overhead is a home run type of shot that we think we should never miss, the fact remains that it's actually one of the most difficult shots in the game. This is especially true if you get careless about setting up for the shot properly, or fail to give it the attention it requires in practice.

Get out and work on the overhead so that you gain the skill and confidence to hit it as hard as you hit the serve. Only by hitting dozens of overheads in a practice session can you learn to gauge when and where to contact that falling ball — by judging its speed and the angle at which it is falling — and to know when to start your upward swing. You should hit with your

A

B

C

100 A–C As the hitter retreats for an overhead, notice how he rotates his non-hitting arm away from the ball and then uncoils as he goes to strike the ball. He sets up properly with his left elbow pointing to the ball (B), but has misjudged the flight of the ball and must lean back as he actually makes contact (C).

same basic serving motion, except that you're concentrating not on a ball toss but on a lob that is falling fast as you go to make contact.

Once you have mastered a basic overhead hitting motion, practice the shot the way you will be expected to perform. Working against a player on the other side of the net who is feeding you a mixture of shots, hit a forehand ground stroke, then an overhead smash, then come in and hit a volley, then retreat for a high backhand volley, and then finish off the point with another overhead smash. Research shows that this random method of practicing is the most effective method for learning to retrieve all the information you have programmed for hitting each of your individual strokes.

Covering Lobs

Always remember that your team is going to have a perilous existence if the two of you are slow to react and retreat when an opponent lobs over you at the net. Conversely, you and your partner will become more aggressive and effective at the net when you know you can turn and run down the best of lobs.

Ideally, for covering excellent deep lobs, spend time practicing the method that gets people from the net to the baseline the fastest, and that's turn and run, like an outfielder in baseball. If you presently backpedal and are reluctant to change, see just how far you can retreat against a lob by the time it reaches the baseline. Then turn and run against the same type of lob. At my tennis college, most players reach the baseline by backpedaling and the back fence by running. Rarely have I seen a player who can backpedal as fast as he can turn and run. Remember, you're running in the direction that you've run all your life — forward — even though you're actually moving away from the net.

I know too that many people are reluctant to play the net because they're afraid they'll get burned by the lob once they are up there. Yet, invariably, I discover they never actually practice retreating for the ball. So I tell my students, "Okay, the moment you see the lob coming, just turn and run toward the fence and don't turn and look for the ball until you hear it bounce on the court." (The lob retriever should know which side the ball is traveling, so that he can turn to the appropriate side when he hears the bounce, ready to hit a return.)

By emphasizing instant reactions ("It's a lob!") and running versus backpedaling, I can get the slowest players to run beyond the baseline and still retrieve a deep lob. And the minute that realization sinks in, they start playing closer to the net for volleys, since they now have confidence they can retreat for lobs. Before, their feared inability to move backward was undermining their volleys. We then go to work on anticipation and learning how to study an opponent's intentions before the ball leaves the racket.

Improving Your Movement to the Ball

Doubles success has a lot to do with time. Overall, you're playing in short bursts — 8, 10 seconds. More specifically, you must learn how to "buy" time to reach as many shots as possible — as early as possible — and how to minimize the time you give

101 A–C This is all the racket movement you need when you go to hit a high volley up at the net. The hitter uses his non-hitting hand to help ensure a short backswing by keeping the racket from going back (A). In photo B, he uses forward body movement for power, not arm movement, and his follow-through is high (C) so that he doesn't hit down on the ball.

A

your opponents to respond to the shots you hit.

Time factors have a greater influence on doubles than on singles because you're constantly in more situations that demand instant decisions and quick movements to the ball. Thus, it pays to practice the skills that will enable you to react and move to the ball with almost preprogrammed instincts against every kind of shot, in a very short time frame.

Many people tell me, "I don't have time to do what you say in doubles." But this skepticism is unwarranted, and to bring it home with my students I have them stand at the net and prepare to volley. Then I tell them, "Quickly turn sideways and put your racket up to volley." How fast is that? Fast enough to allow them to cover a pro-level forehand drive traveling 60 m.p.h. from the baseline. Yet when I then add a ball to the equation — hitting to my students from the baseline — many players are so fearful and anxious about getting hit or just volleying the ball properly that they freeze, instead of quickly moving forward on a diagonal to hit. So as a drill (which I learned from Don Klotz), I start out hitting students soft little shots to volley at the net, and then I increase the speed until they realize they actually have time to volley my hardest forehand drives. The latest brain research seems to support this drill.

If you recognize yourself here, knowing the reality about time recruitment should help reduce your stress out on the court, which in turn should enable you to volley more effectively, because stress tends to inhibit muscle recruitment.

Movement Variations

Movement variations are increasingly cropping up in doubles, fun things you can do to confuse your opponents, such as poaching on every point or every other point, suddenly switching to "one up, one back" position, serving with both players back, or changing court positions. But your team has to practice these desired movements to make them work in a big match. Most teams fail to do this. They get into a

B

C

match and try to do things they haven't done in practice, and it doesn't work.

Also, make sure that your team practices in the same manner you're expected to perform. It has been proved many times by researchers that if the simulator doesn't relate to the thing that you're going to do, then it has no value. If you go out to work on movement drills, the drills should simulate absolutely what you're going to face in a match — both as an individual and as part of a team — so that they become a part of your motor program and there are no confusing surprises.

Here's what I've been emphasizing in recent years. First of all, I truly believe that a doubles team should logically walk through each possible scenario on the court *without their rackets,* with each player providing rationale and discussion points. It's no different from actors rehearsing a play, learning where they must move in relation to one another as they deliver their lines. Actors and doubles players alike must know their "mark" under each condition. After using no rackets, your team should do it again, using rackets to make certain your rackets are up and ready and in the right position. Most teams don't work well as a team because they haven't defined the role and position of each player during a walk-through like this. I would even have "opponents" stand in a particular position on the other side to simulate playing conditions if possible.

After a walk-through, try the drill I learned from Dennis Ralston. You play an unbelievable imagined point, but no ball is hit. You run in for the volley, you run back for a deep overhead, you rush back to the net. Do this drill for one minute, over and over again, and you'll get into great shape.

Anticipation Skills

Anticipation has always been a major emphasis for me, not just because it can help people capitalize on their tennis skills and minimize some of their weaknesses, but because it is directly related to longevity in the sport. When you can accurately anticipate shots, you'll save time and get to the ball sooner, counteracting the speed

A

B

102 A–B When practicing, the player at the net anticipates the down-the-line shot before his opponent strikes the ball (A). He can easily reach any ball hit down the line, three steps away (B).

you might be losing through aging. And, thus, you won't have to be as fast to continue playing the game at your level. You'll also find yourself covering more of the court with less effort, thus easing wear and tear on your body.

My goal is to help maximize your ability to move a quick three steps in any direction, for as photos 102 A–B show, you can cover virtually the whole court — from the center line to the alley — with three steps.

One easy way to improve at getting those quick steps toward the ball is to tackle anticipatory skills, such as how to "read" an opponent's shot before it actually comes off the racket. In reviewing your game, how intently do you actually study your opponent as he or she goes to hit? Are you looking for clues or simply waiting to see where the ball goes before you break in that direction? When your opponents are hitting from the baseline, you should be thinking, "Drive or lob? Drive or lob?" as you study their swing. If it's going to be a drive, try to sense whether it's going down the line or crosscourt. Learn to look at the hitter's front hip, or feet, or any body language that can tip you off to his intentions. Some people will turn a foot, others will turn their head or the lead shoulder — subtle, telltale clues that enable you to break for the ball early.

Personally, I prefer to have my students take their cues from the racket face, since people have a fixed racket position coming into the ball that will not allow them to make a last-second change, irrespective of their body language. Also, it's easy to be distracted by body movements. So when your opponent is hitting the ball, become an expert at reading the racket face, because this is what hits the ball, and racket positions are very revealing.

103 If you were at the net, what would be your movements against each of these players? The girl is lobbing a forehand, the boy is driving a backhand.

Here's where prior charting will help give you an even better sense of anticipating what an opponent is going to do. As I pointed out in chapter 6, you can learn a lot by just sitting in the stands and scouting a team for several games. This will give you objective statistics; and if you're good at anticipation, you'll now have probability theory and visual confirmation on your side.

Gaining a Fast First Step Toward the Ball

Virtually every player in the game can improve at getting a fast first step toward the ball, a skill — especially in doubles — that is much more important than your actual speed afoot. After all, you not only have a partner to share court coverage but also two opponents putting pressure on you to reach the ball quickly.

One of my favorite drills for gaining a fast first step is to have a partner drop a "funny" ball from across the net while you try to follow its movement as it jumps in different directions.

When you go out to play again, keep in mind that you're going to get nervous in a tight match, and this could adversely affect your ability to get a fast first step. While fear is a natural sensation during tough competition, it can also inhibit movement if you're not aware of the dynamics at work. So take a hint from Arthur Ashe, who used to write himself a note — KEEP YOUR FEET MOVING — and leave it at the umpire's stand as a reminder on each changeover. Interesting, I think, that Arthur didn't exhort himself to "stay psyched up." He knew through experience that under pressure the feet go to sleep before the psyche.

Many players could indeed benefit from Ashe's note. They stand on the baseline in doubles, receiving serve, and they fail to move or get a fast first step toward the ball on key points because they're frozen by the pressure. And then you hear them call out: "Play two! I was holding the wrong grip."

Using Videotape

For an amusing and instructive experience, videotape several of your team's matches. If possible, borrow a camera that has fast shutter possibilities, so that it can be stop-framed and still have great clarity. If you can't do this, it will still be a valuable experience. For example, when a camera is stop-framed, a player is either in or out of position. But this revelation should be used to help teams, not to place blame. Often, a camera picks up things the players have never thought about, such as negative body language and recorded comments that stun even the person who made them. Often the camera shows one player constantly trying to control the actions of a partner, which we know is a losing formula. Another common scene is a player who has his or her racket in awkward positions while attacking the net, resulting in being late for the hit.

Improving your team's performance will take time and patience as you try to incorporate smarter tactics while concentrating on better technique with each stroke. After several practice sessions — or perhaps after even a week away at a tennis camp — you'll likely have high expectations in your first big match. But things may not go well, and, with confidence dwindling, you're apt to fall back on comfortable old habits, such as failing to get a fast first step toward the ball. But stick to the improvements you are seeking to master and don't be derailed, for you'll soon be reaping the benefits and will find yourself on the next-higher level of play.

Just as in singles, remember that doubles always comes down to the same thing: Know what shot you have to hit under each condition, practice these shots, and make your best effort to hit them in a match. This already makes you a winner in my book. If you win the match, you are a double winner. Beyond that, I like players to be observant about their playing levels. If you study the game and work hard and keep moving up, don't be afraid to pat yourself on the back, win or lose. Improvement is something to take pride in.

CHAPTER 10

Coping with All the Variables

NOW that you're on the road to becoming a great doubles player (even if your domain ends at the county line), you're always going to be in demand, and your skills will help you win with a variety of players, men and women alike.

Everybody loves to play with a person who has experience in doubles and knows how the game ought to be played, somebody who can quickly fall into sync with another veteran player after just a brief exchange. For example, if you pair up, sight unseen, with an experienced doubles player, the very first time he prepares to serve, you should be able to say, "Look, I like to poach on ad if you're down the middle," and he will understand this shorthand. Next, ask this question: Does he follow his serve to the net, or does he leave you up there alone? Then you can start worrying about his on-court temperament.

If you're an itinerant doubles player, always entering various events here and there, or a relative newcomer to the game, seeking out a permanent partner, you'll find yourself playing with a variety of new partners in different types of competition at the club and around town. Doubles is your game, whenever there's an opportunity. This means you must adjust to various personalities and playing styles from week to week, season to season, and if you plan to have fun while playing your own style of tennis, you must stand up for yourself, be flexible, not take things personally — and retain a sense of humor.

No doubt about it, no matter how many years you play doubles, you're continually going to encounter wonderful partners and opponents but also bizarre individuals who have irritating habits that will drive you nuts unless you are prepared to accept their antics as just part of the game. For example, what about the person who grunts as she swings, à la Monica Seles? Or the partner who has a way of saying "Out!" that begins to infuriate your opponents and makes you uncomfortable? Or the opponent who likes to bounce the ball nine times before serving? She actually controls you, because if you try to walk away or look away and she decides to serve after the seventh bounce, you're tap city.

Obviously you simply have to go with the flow.

Typical Doubles Situations

Here are other situations that likely will arise when you walk out onto the court with relative strangers — and some appropriate reactions on your part.

Left Side, Right Side

Most people know which side of the court they prefer to play — left or right, ad or deuce — and ideally you will hook up with someone who likes to play your less effective, less favorite side. If you both want to play the same side, you can flip a coin or let the more aggressive person decide, but the key determinant (assuming you're both right-handed) should be this: Who has the most consistent service return? That person should play the *right* side, unless he's also the more aggressive net player and likes to poach. Most stronger players, even if they have a better service return than their partners, still prefer to play the left side because they like the net action moving left to right and they enjoy hitting the overheads that come down the middle.

In a game where most rallies are over by the third or fourth shot, you want a person returning serve who can get you into the point. If the right-court player can hit a strong return at deuce, low and away from the net player, then the pressure is on the server to volley effectively and put the pressure back on your team.

If it's important to know who has the best overall service return, here's a good drill. Have a strong server hit a variety of serves to you and your partner — hard, flat serves; hard serves with spin; off-speed serves; kick serves — and find out which person is best overall at returning them. Placement and consistency are the key determinants.

Remember, if your partner plays the right court and can help your team win a lot of points at deuce, he or she gives you the ad — and there's much less pressure riding on your weaker return. You can think to yourself, "If I don't get the ball back or if it goes right to the net person, that's okay; it's just deuce again." This should free you to hit out with your best attempt and not baby the ball just to get it back in play.

Also reiterating what I said earlier in the book: You and your partner should be practical and flexible about positioning, reflecting your individual styles of play. For example, in most partnerships, the steadier player should play the right side, taking pride in keeping the ball in play and setting up his partner — the flashier player — at the net. Also, the stronger singles player is usually best suited as the left-court player, but again, this isn't an automatic decision.

In mixed doubles, I've rarely seen a woman playing the backhand side anywhere in the world, which is a strategic mistake in many cases. I've long argued that a strong woman club player paired with a lower-rated male should often take the left side. This is a hard tradition to break, however, since most players think a mixed-doubles team lives and dies with the left-court player, and what woman is going to move aside the macho male? Also, I think the right-handed male player — if he's noticeably taller — feels he can poach more effectively moving left to right and can take all overheads down the middle.

When I asked Brain Typing expert Jonathan Niednagel for his advice about right-court, left-court pairings, he had these comments:

> There are some exceptions, of course, but introverted people are more apt to be defensive, while extroverted people are more likely to be aggressive and offensive-thinking. Introverted, left-brain people should play the right side: they are more structured, organized, defensive-minded individuals, and they're quite happy to just "hit it back" like a returning device. In contrast, the high-energy, extroverted right-brain person is not content to just stand there and methodically return the ball; he wants to take the service return and try to score off of it.
>
> So ideally, in terms of meshing tennis skills, the extroverted right-brain person should team with an introverted left-brain person — providing they can get along, personality-wise. Chris Evert gained her fame playing singles, but in doubles she would have been a classic right-court player, without a doubt. But she should never be paired with a person like herself.

The same thinking would apply to a player like Ken Rosewall. He was kind of an introverted guy; it was hard to get him to talk, but he was one of the greatest right-handers ever to play the right side because he never missed on the service return and he had a great volley as well. What a team he formed with Lew Hoad roaming the left side.

The Desired Criteria for a Woman in Mixed Doubles

In mixed doubles, the required qualities for a good player are the same for men and women alike. Yet despite the fact that many women players are much better than their male partners, people still ask me, "What are the qualities needed for a woman to play with a macho man against a team with another macho male?" Here are my criteria:

1. A good serve — not necessarily hard but consistently deep and in play.
2. A reliable service return, away from the net person as often as possible.
3. A sharp, aggressive volley, so she can play the net and poach.
4. An overhead, with the emphasis on accuracy over power.

Good forehands and backhands off the ground, after the service return, don't mean as much in strong tournament play because few rallies last long enough to demand a ground stroke from the baseline, and both teams are striving to play at the net.

The Control Freak

Psychologically, it's a natural human phenomenon: We all have our own particular control system, a desired playing style and comfortable mannerisms we're reluctant to give up when we play doubles.

The brain's control system doesn't want to yield control to another system, another person, but compromise is an integral part of the teamwork exchange in good doubles. Recognizing these dynamics at work, the question becomes, Can you give up half of your control while your partner gives up half? Both of you must compromise to play well together. Moreover, you must try to give up the half that's your more detrimental side, while retaining the best aspects and not be scared off by your partner's particular personality and style of play.

The control freak gives himself away in a number of ways. A skilled older woman told me that in a pickup match at her club, she drew a man who insisted on keeping the second ball when she served, even though she had served quite well for 40 years holding the second ball herself. He insisted on feeding them to her one at a time, but took an inordinately long time to do so, slowing up play and quietly infuriating even the opponents. She asked me what she should have done, and I told her, "Well, you're right, he was a jerk, but he's the type of person who *has* to control his partner's action. He was telling you, in effect, 'I don't care what you want when you serve; here's what I want when you serve.' You should have asked him, 'I'm curious — why do you want to hold the second ball? Why is this important?' And then whatever his answer — perhaps he felt that you had too small a hand to hold two balls on the first toss — you could have responded, 'Well, I serve best when I hold two balls, so I'm going to hold two balls.'" What counts is that there be freedom to discuss and, I hope, room for compromise.

When answers are unsatisfactory, try to keep your friendship with your partner as you explain that doubles means something else to you and you're basically saying "Adios" to this matchup.

The Partner who Refuses to Play the Net

While in Argentina on a teaching mission, I once came across a fellow who insisted he had to serve from in front of the back fence because he couldn't get his serve in from the baseline. At first I thought he was joking, but on every point he would start at the baseline, then turn and move backward before serving. I guess he felt he had to start at the baseline. He actually could get the ball in, but his partner up at the net certainly didn't get much help.

Gigantic arguments can arise in doubles when one person refuses to play the net and his partner refuses to play at the baseline (unless forced to do so by a lob). In a stalemate like this, nobody wins unless each player agrees to compromise with a "one up, one back" system, which is ultimately a losing system. So, if you acquire a partner who loves to stay back and you thrive at the net, you must first try to convince him that your team's chances of winning are much greater if you *both* go to the net at every opportunity. If he still insists on staying back — and wants you to join him — don't cave in and let him control your preferred style of play. Instead, realize that you now have it all, that you can actually play the whole front court — from net post to net post — without any guilt, providing you have the quickness, stamina, and volleying skills required. Play up there and cut off every ball you can;

104 At the pro level, the receiving team is forced to have one player back (the receiver) and one player up against a team where the server moves in behind his serve. Now all the pressure is on the receiver to execute. *(Photo: Lisa Marie Roberto)*

105 If you're up at the net and you have a partner who's stuck on the baseline or simply won't come to the net, be ready to poach on the very next shot. Get up on your toes as your opponent goes to drive the ball, then break toward the center stripe. If you anticipate correctly, you will be able to cut off his crosscourt attempt with a putaway volley.

and if your partner begins to complain that he's not getting many shots, tell him what I've emphasized in this book: The closest player to the net has priority, from net post to net post.

Meanwhile, if your partner wants to win this particular match, or if this is a partnership the two of you somehow want to preserve, he must go along with the strategy you've chosen by protecting your backside, covering for your poaches and your across-the-court volleying efforts. Yet he can also enjoy roaming the backcourt area to hit ground strokes.

While this modified "one up, one back" system is still almost always doomed against a team that moves up to the net together, good poaching can keep you in the match. What you must do, though, is establish signals so that you can go in the middle of a point, confident that your partner will cover your backside. Just an easy arrangement such as, "Elbows in, I'm staying put; elbows out, I'm going on the next one," or, "If my foot is up, or if I touch my racket to the court, I'm going." When you're at the net and ready to poach, just wait for your opponent to drop his eyes as he goes to hit, then take off. Your partner should break at the same moment and cover the opposite side of the baseline.

By playing this way, you will no longer be controlled by a partner who loves the baseline. Instead of brooding to yourself, "I'm going to just get killed up here," you're now free to go all day long, whenever you want. Moreover, you're disrupting the other team. At first, when they realize that your partner is always going to stay back, they'll be filled with optimism, knowing they can win the match by constantly crowding the net as a team. But now, if you can pose a constant threat at the net — as a regular volleyer and as a poacher — they have a less predictable and more difficult task trying to capitalize on gaps in your team's defense.

Playing Up or Playing Down

If you have trouble adjusting to playing with people at the playing level immediately above you or below you, try to bow out of these situations ahead of time by avoiding certain tournament events where players of varying abilities are thrown together. Instead of entering a fund-raising event and then complaining all afternoon — "I'm an A player and I have to play with a toad" — do everybody a favor ahead of time by sending the organizers a check. Then come out if you want and watch the fun, but don't feel you have to play. You don't owe anyone an apology. If, instead, you try to play when you're miserable, your partner can read your body language and will not only feel bad but will tend to play worse, and so you will help kill other people's fun.

When you get stuck in a situation where you are clearly the best player, don't try to show off your superior skills or "baby" everything you hit. Instead, concentrate on returning every shot that comes your way and spend time experimenting on strokes, so that you come out of the match having learned something. This is a wonderful time to practice looking at the ball, or keeping your head still as you swing, or striving to move forward constantly.

When you're the weakest of four players, try to take the same approach. Remember, the very best you can do is execute, no matter whom you play with, so tell yourself, "I'm just going to focus on getting the ball back the best I can, even if I never win a point for my team." This is tough, I know, but without this focus you'll find yourself hitting everything into the net or out of play when you're thrown in with better players.

Avoiding Player X

If you're going to be playing in an open-ended club or charity event and there's a certain player you would like to avoid as a partner, get in touch with the tournament committee before you're committed to play, so that they have time to adjust the pairings. Tell the chairman, "Here's my problem — I can't play with this person; we've had problems in the past and playing together just wouldn't be pleasant." If the chairman tells you, "Well, it could come up; we can't control the pairings," then you should pass on the event and not cause tournament-day headaches for the committee with your complaining in the event you are indeed paired up with this person. If you wait, there's no graceful way to bow out and you will ruin the pairings.

I know how this can all come about from personal experience. I once organized the opening ceremonies for a tennis club in Los Angeles, and we had several movie stars lined up to play doubles. I knew that one of these stars was fiercely competitive and loved to win, no matter what the circumstances, so I paired him with Beverly Baker Fleitz, a former national doubles champ and Wimbledon singles finalist. Unfortunately, this actor also truly believed he could play the game, but on this particular night he played lousy and Baker Fleitz had to pull off every trick to make sure they won, legitimately "stealing" many of his shots at the net and up the middle.

I had known this actor for a long time, and when I saw him afterward, I felt sure he was going to tell me how much fun he had had with Baker Fleitz. Instead, he was steaming and he told me off something fierce: "Don't ever put me with a woman again!"

Well, obviously I should have told the fellow beforehand, "Look, if there's anybody you don't want to play with, let me know because we're just having some fun — nothing too serious." But I assumed he would love to play with a Wimbledon veteran like Baker Fleitz, who would have whipped his butt in singles and was a nice person to boot.

Sticking to Your Playing System

Since strategy and shot selection are quite predictable in good doubles, it's easy to acquire a playing "system" that you can take from match to match anywhere in the country. The problem comes, of course, when you get paired with the person who wants to camp at the baseline, or with somebody who whispers before the first point, "Watch your alley," instead of focusing on the fact that most shots will be coming down the middle in most rallies. Or with the person who advises you, "Never lob," when actually a good lob can serve as a lethal weapon.

When you have worked on a system and you get paired with somebody who contaminates the system (e.g., by asking you to stay back when he serves, instead of starting at the "X" in the middle of the service box), try to realize that this person is sending you tremendously mixed messages. In one sense he's admitting to stroking deficiencies, such as in his serve or his volley, but he's also a controlling individual who will usually be more concerned about dictating your team's strategy than actually winning the match. Basically, you must respond in a positive way, designed to help your team indeed win the match.

For example, instead of trying to adjust to his weak serve by staying back at the baseline, insist that you are going to play the net and do what the partner of the server should try to do: Cut off the service return at the net. Let him know you are going to stay up there and take a shot at it and not hang back with him. He may get mad, because he wants to control the situation, but you have to hold your ground if you want to play doubles the way it ought to be played. (Conversely, if you prefer to stay back and your partner wants to play at the net, reassure him that you want him up there, because it's not fair or wise to take away your partner's strength just because of your weakness. That's the part of giving in doubles that I've stressed in this book.)

"Stay on Your Side of the Line"

In chapter 6, I noted that you'll know you're in trouble if your new partner tries to tell you before the match, "See that center stripe? That's your side and this is my side. Never get on my side."

If you want to win, or at least enjoy playing doubles correctly, stand tough. Remind this person that while you respect his apparent, but still unproven, ability to play his side of the court and respond to shots down the middle, you subscribe to the adage that the person closest to the net has priority on all shots down the middle, even if that means crossing into his territory to take the shot.

In fact, if you run in front of your partner at the net and hit a volley, the problem is not you — it's your partner, because you were where your partner was supposed to be.

Treat Her Like a Lady?

In mixed doubles today, despite the fact that many women are every bit the equal of men at the net, the question still frequently arises: How should the woman across the net be treated? Should you attack or give her space?

My advice is to respect her just like a male opponent. If you can't volley to an open area on the court, then go for her right hip, because that handcuffs her quite well — just as long as your intent is simply to win the point, not also to hurt or intimidate the person.

At the pro level, University of Southern California coach Dick Leach offered this perspective to sportswriter Joe Jares in 1990, after his son, Rick, won Wimbledon titles with Jim Pugh and Zina Garrison:

> The girls think that the guys enjoy playing mixed, but that's not true. They're playing for only one reason — money. It's hard work. It's damned if you do and damned if you don't. You have to poach all the time and you're at the mercy of the woman. If she plays well, you win. If she plays lousy, you lose. You just have to be an animal out there if you want to win.
>
> It's the guy who wants to drill the female the most. And one of the reasons I think Ricky doesn't do better is because he doesn't go after the other gal, he doesn't try to smack balls at her, he doesn't play aggressively enough. At Wimbledon this year, I was all over him before every match. I said, "The other guy's going to be pumping balls at Zina [Garrison]. Are you going to go after it or are you going to sit back and play 50-50 doubles?"
>
> He was very animated, and he won.

(The elder Leach, incidentally, was involved in the longest official doubles match in history. He and partner Dick Dell outlasted Tom Mozur and Len Schloss 3–6, 49–47, 22–20 in a tournament at the Newport Casino in 1967. That's more than 14 sets of 6–4 tennis! The match had to be completed over a two-day period and was only the semi-finals. "As soon as we finished," Leach recalls, "we had to go back out and play the finals against Jim McManus and Jim Osborne, and we went 6–8, 8–6, 8–6. The next day we were in bed all day, frozen. And I could barely walk.")

Personality Factors

If you're concerned about having an on-court personality that will appeal to most of your potential partners, men and women alike, measure yourself against this checklist of common complaints that I've heard over the years about doubles partners (supplemented by a survey that appeared in *Playgirl* magazine):

1. Complains too much and tends to give up.
2. Constantly apologizes for poor shots.
3. Hits too many poking, pushing, dinking shots.
4. Has trouble seeing the lines and makes too many obviously wrong calls, which is embarrassing.
5. Is too timid about going for her shots at the net.
6. Often gives up on the next shot after missing a shot.
7. Takes too much time in between points and games.
8. Is a hotdogger with a bad temper.
9. Has a "superior jock" attitude.
10. Cannot serve holding two balls.
11. Tries to play the whole court, even when it's unwarranted.
12. Plays for blood — is too argumentative and talkative.
13. Lacks aggression; always wants to move back.

On the other hand, here are some of the common characteristics displayed by players who are always in demand as doubles partners:

1. Plays hard while also enjoying the game.
2. Is aggressive and knows tactics.
3. Keeps the ball in play.
4. Allows me to make my own shot, when warranted.
5. Is not afraid to make mistakes.
6. Has a sense of humor.
7. Always tries, no matter what his playing level.
8. Strives to play her proper position on the court.
9. Has the ability to cover his own area and responsibilities.
10. Doesn't apologize for every missed shot.
11. Hangs in all the way.
12. Applauds good shots by the opponents.
13. Shows support when I'm playing lousy. Never says, "Just get the damn ball in the court; I'll do the rest."

Practicing Your Skills

If you're determined to become a better doubles player, think about your different responsibilities and practice them; get them ingrained in your mind so you don't have to think during a point. Each little concept that's important in doubles must be practiced, yet, as I have emphasized, most players fail to set aside this time. People tell me, "I know what you're saying, Vic. I'll think about it at home, then just do it when I play." But you're not going to pull it off in a match without some prior rehearsal on the court. If you wait to try out all of your new tricks when you're playing a big match, you're going to run cut of partners.

Now don't get me wrong. You never want to be afraid to experiment and make mistakes as you play; you want to learn something from every match. But first set up a practice session where you have specific goals in mind. For instance, "Today I will practice taking balls down the center and I will work on getting close to the net. I'm going to keep my feet moving. I'm going to work on anticipating my opponent's shot. I'm going to keep my eyes

106 When your opponent has a putaway overhead right across the net, don't try to challenge him. Instead, turn your back to the shot and avoid injury.

down on the ball when I make my hit, and try to block out my opponents. Then I am going to work on getting my first serve in play so that my partner won't have to wear a helmet."

Good Doubles Etiquette

The "rules" of doubles etiquette have evolved over the years. They are unwritten but understood among experienced players. Here are several examples:

- In good doubles, when you're in a vulnerable position near the net — for example, the opponent has a putaway overhead right in front of you — it's your responsibility to turn your back as a sign of submission so that he can relax and hit safely around you. If you try to distract your opponent instead of turning away, then you must accept the consequences, like taking a ball in the face. Your opponent is not required to hit around you if you stand there and challenge him because very often when a person tries to miss people, he misses his shot.
- If you call "out" on a shot and your partner says, "No, that was good," the proper etiquette (it's part of the rules) is to give your opponents the point. In fact, if one person thinks that the shot was good, then it probably was. Our research shows

107 When both teams play hard and enjoy the competition, it's hard to tell which team is the winner. *(Photo: Lisa Marie Roberto)*

that a ball compresses when it hits the ground and slides a couple of inches before leaving the ground. Players normally see the take off point rather than the landing point, so even if a shot looks slightly out, a part of the ball probably hit the line before rebounding off the court.

• What to do about an opponent with "two-inch" eyes? You know, the player who on every close call says, "Sorry, but your shot was out by just two inches." He tends to get away with it because he seems to have such remarkable eyesight and he sounds so convincing. Similarly, we've all played against the team that suffers from "out-itis," a compulsive tendency to call "out" on all close line shots by their opponents.

Unfortunately, there's not much you can do about players like this, unless you're in a tournament situation, where you can request a linesperson. I've found that challenging a player's constant bad calls usually only irritates the victim, because the victim is not accustomed to this cheating and the player with "bad eyes" never changes the call. So my advice would be that (1) you try to get a linesperson, (2) if you already know about this person, you ask for a linesperson before the match begins, or (3) you simply say to the cheater, "I'm disappointed with the way you call lines, and I'll simply hold up the number of fingers for the times I think you've hooked me." This sometimes gets to the other player.

- When it comes to a team's behavior on the court, always keep in mind that there are players who never complain about their partner but who are very self-abusive. This practice is as disruptive and unsettling to everybody as yelling at a partner.

Whoever your partner might be, and whatever the circumstances of the match, try to put aside fears of failure as you simply concentrate on the competition at hand, because fear is a major psychological reason people don't play as well as they should. When people are frightened about "looking bad," their whole goal is to play it safe, avoid their weak areas, and skirt unfamiliar strategy. Instead, you should be out there focused on the play, playing hard and having a good time. Why not play doubles simply because it's *fun?* You have a chance to laugh, you meet people, you compete in a great sport. You obviously can't play well all the time — you're going to play crummy at times — but you can always try to play your best despite what's going on around you. Sure, winning is the point of the game, but why view the sport as a win-or-else arena when we already know the statistics? Fifty percent of the people who play tennis on a given day will lose. But everybody wins if you know how to have fun and enjoy the game. When you play with this philosophy, the winner has fun, plus he wins; the loser still has fun. He gets one out of two, and that's worth something in our win-at-all-costs society.

A Doubles Glossary

(This alphabetical listing explains the basic tennis and teaching terms used in this book, as well as some others you may encounter as you get involved in playing doubles.)

Ace A ball served so well it goes untouched by the opponent's racket.

Ad Short for *advantage.*

Ad service court When serving or returning serve, the left side as a player faces the net. (See court diagram in chap. 4.)

Advantage A scoring term referring to the lead held by the side that wins the first point after deuce — e.g., "advantage Phillips/Crawford."

All A scoring term that refers to an equal score for both players or sides — e.g., "30-all."

Alley The $4\frac{1}{2}$-foot strip on each side of the court used during doubles play. The two doubles alleys enlarge the court from a 27-foot width for singles to a 36-foot width for doubles. (See court diagram in chap. 4.)

Angle The direction of a player's shot in relation to any line parallel to, and including, the baseline (measured in degrees).

Anticipation The ability to make educated guesses as to the type, speed, direction, and elevation of an opponent's shot before the shot has been made.

Approach shot Any shot used to approach or gain position at the net, but typically a ball from near the midcourt area, after which the hitter continues forward toward the net.

Attack To take the offensive rather than play defensive tennis. Most offensive tennis involves moving in from the baseline at every opportunity — attacking (rushing) the net — and quick, aggressive net play.

Backcourt The area on the playing court bounded by the service line, the baseline, and the sidelines. (See court diagram in chap. 4.)

Backhand The stroke used by right-handers to hit balls on their left side and left-handers to hit balls on their right side. The body pivot automatically turns the back side of the hitting hand toward the net.

Backhand corner The corner of the playing court to which one must run to hit a backhand.

Backpedal To run backward while facing the net.

Backswing The beginning part of a stroke: the movement of the hitting arm and racket backward to a position from which the downward or forward motion begins.

Baseline The boundary line at each end of the playing court, located 39 feet from the net. (See court diagram in chap. 4.)

Break point The situation when the server is within one point of losing the game in which he is serving.

Break serve To win a game in which the opponent is the server. (See also *Hold serve*.)

Center line The playing-court line on both sides of the net (and the line perpendicular to it) that separates the service courts. (See court diagram in chap. 4.)

Center mark The short slash ("hash mark") on the playing court that bisects each baseline. (See court diagram in chap. 4.)

Center strap A strap placed at the middle of the net and anchored to the court to maintain a 3-foot net height at the center line.

Charting Gathering and recording statistics on errors, placements, and other pertinent details of a match.

Check step A footwork technique used when attacking the net that involves bringing both feet together momentarily as the player determines the direction of an opponent's shot. Also called a split step or stutter step.

Chip The short, high-to-low forward motion of the racket as it contacts the lower back side of the ball to impart underspin. Also, a shot hit in this manner, or to hit such a shot.

Close off the point To move aggressively and hit offensive shots at the right opportunity (e.g., when an opponent is out of position) in order to end the point quickly.

Conceal shots To hit shots without revealing their intended speed, direction, or elevation in advance.

Court The playing surface. (See court diagram in chap. 4.)

Crosscourt shot A ball hit diagonally from one corner or side of the court, over the net, to the opposite corner or side (rather than down the line or down the middle).

Crossover The periodic switch of players from one side of the court to the other during competition to equalize the effect of sun, wind, and other peripheral factors.

Cut off the angle To move forward quickly (when volleying) against an opponent's crosscourt shot in order to hit the ball before the angle gets wider or the ball moves deeper into your court.

Deep shot A ground stroke or volley that bounces inbounds near the opponent's baseline, or a serve that lands in play near the service line.

Deuce A scoring term that refers to a game score of 40-40 or any tied game score beyond that point.

Deuce service court When serving or returning serve, the right side as a player faces the net. (See court diagram in chap. 4.)

Double-fault To lose a point by making two consecutive unsuccessful serves (the unforced error is called a double fault).

Doubles sideline The outermost side boundary on each side of the playing court, located at the ends of the baseline and perpendicular to it. Used in doubles only. (See court diagram in chap. 4.)

Down-the-line shot A ball hit from near a sideline that travels along that line rather than down the middle or crosscourt.

Down-the-middle shot A ball, usually hit from the midcourt or backcourt, that travels along the center of the court rather than down the line or crosscourt.

Drive An offensive ground stroke (usually in a baseline rally).

Drive volley A high volley hit very hard with an unusual amount of backswing.

Drop shot An off-speed ground stroke, hit in such a manner that it drops just over the net with little or no forward bounce. This shot is designed to win a point outright or to tire an opponent who is behind the baseline or off to one side of the court.

Drop volley A volley hit in such a manner that it drops just barely over the net with little or no forward bounce. Also called a stop volley.

Earned point A point won as a result of a forced error.

Fast court A playing surface such as cement that causes the ball to skid off it quickly.

Fault An unsuccessful serve — usually one that fails to land inside the proper service court. (See also *Double-fault; Foot fault.*)

F.B.I. "First ball in" on the serve counts (i.e., more than two faults are allowed) when a player is serving for the first time in the match. This is never acceptable in official tennis.

Fifteen In scoring, the first point scored by a player or a side. Also called "five" erroneously.

Five See *Fifteen.*

Flat shot A ball hit with very little spin.

Foot fault A serve that's disallowed because of improper foot movement. Foot faults are usually committed by stepping on the baseline or onto the court before the ball has been contacted, but they can also be committed by running along the baseline before serving.

Forced error An error that is induced by one player's strong play, such as failing to return a shot that has been hit so hard or at such a sharp angle that there's insufficient time to respond with a normal stroke.

Forecourt The area on each side of the playing court bounded by the net, the service line, and the sidelines. (See court diagram in chap. 4.)

Forehand corner The corner of the playing court to which one must run to hit a forehand.

Forty In scoring, the third point won by a player or side.

Grip The manner in which a player grasps the racket handle, e.g., the Eastern forehand or backhand, the Continental, the Western, or the semi-Western.

Groove strokes Uniform, consistent strokes — ideally, proper ones that can be relied upon under pressure.

Ground stroke A shot in which the ball is hit after it has bounced (as opposed to a volley).

Half-volley A stroke in which the ball is contacted only inches away from the court's surface after it has bounced. (It should more accurately be called a "half-ground stroke.")

"Hit deep" To hit ground strokes that consistently land in play near the opponent's baseline.

"Hit out" To make a complete and uninhibited swing at the ball, whatever the pressure.

Hitting zone The short distance in the racket path just before and including the impact point during which the ball can be hit on line with the intended target.

"Hit up" To hit the ball on an upward trajectory (on ground strokes, serves, and overheads).

Hold serve To win a game while serving. (See also *Break serve.*)

In play A valid shot, hit inbounds, that will win the point unless returned by the opponent.

Left service court (or box) See *Ad service court.*

Let ball Any point that is played over because of interference of some nature (such as a ball that rolls across the court from an adjoining one).

Let serve A serve that touches the net tape before landing in the proper service box. Let serves are replayed and do not count as a fault.

Line call An announcement that a shot has landed out of bounds.

Lob A ground stroke hit sufficiently high to pass over the outstretched racket of an opponent at the net. Used primarily to drive an opponent away from the net or to buy time to get back into position on the court.

Lob volley A shot hit high into the air from a volleying position.

Long ball A shot that lands out of bounds beyond the baseline.

Love The score of a player (or team) who has either won no points in a game or no games in a set.

Match A contest between two opponents (or two pairs of players) that is complete when one side wins a specified number of sets (normally either two or three).

Match point The situation when one player (or team) will win the match if he can win the next point.

Midcourt The area on each side of the playing court near the service line. (See court diagram in chap. 4.)

Mix up shots To change the speed, elevation, and spin of shots constantly to confuse an opponent's anticipation and rhythm.

Net ball A shot that hits the net and falls back on the same side as the hitter.

Net player One who has gained position at the net and is prepared to volley.

Offensive lob A ball hit just above the racket reach of an opposing net player, normally driven hard with topspin.

Opening An opportunity to hit to where the opposing player has left a wide gap.

Open stance A hitting position in which the feet and belly button point toward the net (which prevents a player from stepping in to the ball).

Overhead A forehand stroke hit while the ball is higher than one's head.

Overhit To tend to put too much force into a shot by hitting hard without corresponding control.

Overplay To favor one side of the court, generally as a tactic against a particular opponent, but also to compensate for one's own particular weakness — e.g., to overplay the forehand or backhand side.

Pace The speed of the ball.

Passing shot A ball hit in play from the baseline that passes beyond the reach of a player at the net or approaching it.

Pattern tennis A sequence of shot selections that has been planned before the match and that is repeated frequently. For many players, this helps reduce the need for excessive thinking during a match.

Placement A shot hit so accurately (and usually with good pace) that it goes untouched by the opponent — e.g., an ace.

Poach To move early into the partner's territory to volley an opponent's service return or ground stroke rally shot.

Ready position The relaxed posture a player should assume as he awaits his opponent's hit so that he can take the fastest possible first step toward the ball.

Receiver The player to whom the ball is being served.

Retrieve To reach an opponent's well-placed shot and get it back over the net and in play.

Right service court (or box) See *Deuce service court.*

Run around a shot To intentionally avoid hitting a particular stroke.

Rush the net To move in aggressively from the baseline and try to capitalize on an opponent's weak shot. (See also *Attack.*)

Safety margin The distance by which the ball clears the net tape and lands in the desired spot.

Serve The stroke that puts the ball in play on every point.

Server The player initiating play. The server is given two chances to land the ball in his opponent's service court; failing that, he loses the point. (See also *Fault.*)

Service court (or box) The rectangular area on the court in which a serve must land to be valid. The boundaries of the four service courts are formed by the net, the singles sidelines, the service lines, and the center line. (See also *Ad service court; Deuce service court;* court diagram in chap. 4.)

Service line The back boundary of the service courts, which runs parallel to the net.

Service return The stroke used to return a serve.

Set A contest made up of a group of games that is complete when one player or side wins at least six while holding a minimum two-game lead. (See also *Match; Tiebreaker.*)

Set point The last point needed to win a set.

Setup A ball hit so softly and close to the net that after it bounces the opponent is "set up."

Short-angle shot A ball that clears the net traveling crosscourt, away from the opponent, and, normally, falls within the service court. This shot can be hit hard, but most players take the speed off.

Short ball Any shot except the serve that lands less deep than intended, generally giving the opponent an offensive opportunity.

Short-ball range The distance on the court a player can cover after hitting an approach shot and still reach his desired "X" position for volleying, as or before his opponent strikes the ball.

Sideline See *Singles sideline; Doubles sideline.*

Sidespin A ball hit with horizontal rotation. (See also *Slice.*)

Singles sideline The innermost side boundary on each side of the playing court, perpendicular to the net and running the entire length of the court. Used in singles play. (See court diagram in chap. 4.)

Slice On the serve or the overhead, a ball struck by a racket face that is moving sideways as it contacts the outer back side of the ball, thus producing sidespin.

Slow court A playing surface such as clay that causes the ball to rebound slowly and rather high.

Spin Rotation imparted to the ball that affects how it curves and bounces.

Split step See *Check step.*

Stop volley See *Drop volley.*

Strategy A player's master plan for winning, carefully formulated before a match to give him the best chance at beating a particular opponent.

Stutter step See *Check step.*

"Take two" A term used following an interference in play; a courteous opponent will suggest that the server "take two" — start the point over with two serve attempts allowed.

Target line A straight line between the hitter's racket and his intended target.

Telegraph shots To inadvertently reveal to an opponent the intended speed, direction, or elevation of one's shots before hitting them.

Tiebreaker A scoring method commonly used in tournament play to end a set when the score reaches 6–6. The most widely accepted version is the 12-point system, in which the winner is the first player to win 7 points and be ahead by at least 2 points. The player whose turn it is to serve initiates the first point, and thereafter the opponents alternate the serve after every two points.

Topspin Ball rotation on a vertical axis that causes the ball to arc downward and bounce high.

"T" position The place on each side of the playing court where the center line meets the service line. (See court diagram in chap. 4.)

Underspin Ball rotation on a horizontal axis imparted by contacting the lower back side of the ball with a racket moving from high to low. (Also called backspin.)

Unearned point A point won as the result of an unforced error.

Unforced error An error that is the result of one player's weak play rather than an opponent's skill, such as a setup that's knocked into the net.

"Up and out" An important concept on the serve and overhead: The racket head should be going skyward and away from a player's head as it approaches the ball and after impact.

Vertical racket face A racket hitting surface that is straight up and down at impact (as if resting on its edge on a table), on a plane parallel to the net.

Volley A shot in which the ball is hit before it has bounced (as opposed to a ground stroke).

"X" position The spot on the court a player wants to reach after hitting an approach shot — located several feet to either side of the center line, in the direction of the shot and halfway between the service line and the net. This "X" position places the volleyer about halfway between where most opponents can hit passing shots either down the line or crosscourt.